IN CONFIDENCE

Roberta Israeloff

IN CONFIDENCE:
FOUR YEARS
of THERAPY

HOUGHTON MIFFLIN COMPANY

Boston 1990

For information about permission to reproduce selections from
this book, write to Permissions, Houghton Mifflin Company,
2 Park Street, Boston, Massachusetts 02108.

Library of Congress Cataloging-in-Publication Data

Israeloff, Roberta, date.
    In confidence : four years of therapy / Roberta Israeloff
        p.   cm.
    ISBN 0–395–47101–X
    1. Israeloff, Roberta, date — Mental health.   2. Psychotherapy
patients — United States — Biography.   I. Title.
RC464.I87A3   1990
616.89'14'092 — dc20   89–35545
[B]   CIP

Printed in the United States of America

Q 10 9 8 7 6 5 4 3 2 1

Included in this book are portraits of many people, both friends
and relations, who had an effect on my therapy. With the ex-
ception of my husband, my son, and my parents, the names
and identifying characteristics of all individuals have been
changed in order to protect their privacy.

For David,
Ellen,
and my therapist

This book has had a long gestation, during which I received much encouragement from my friends and family, and I thank them. I would also like to thank Diane Cole for her generous advice and support, and Helen Benedict, Katrina Kenison, and Toinette Lippe for their help with the nascent manuscript. To Larry Kessenich and Frances Kiernan, I owe a special debt of gratitude for their vision and guidance; and finally, to Lynn Seligman, continuing thanks.

THE FIRST YEAR

I

THE PSYCHOLOGIST, a tall, middle-aged woman wearing enormous tortoiseshell glasses and smoking a cigarette, her brown hair swept up in a bun, approached me in the crowded waiting room. We shook hands as if we were strangers meeting at a train station. Then she led me to a room that had the most luxurious chair I had ever sat in: it swiveled and reclined, and I felt swaddled in its comfort. Nearby on a table was a box of Kleenex and a small digital clock angled so that I couldn't see its face. She sat in a similar chair across from me, stubbed out her cigarette, and began the preliminary interview by asking me why I was seeking therapy.

Her question unsettled me. A month ago, when I had first called the Institute and requested an appointment, I had been sent an application form whose last section posed the same question. I had spent two days carefully composing my answer. Hadn't this woman seen my file? "Yes, it's right there," she assured me, gesturing toward a folder on the table. But now she wanted me to talk through my reasons.

I tried to recite my essay from memory: Therapy was for my son's sake. Although I had always characterized my own childhood as happy and my parents as loving, caring, and well-meaning, they nevertheless had trouble understanding me. I wanted to be the kind of parent who understood. I wanted to allow my child the opportunity to grow up without feeling as if a struggle was waging within him, the kind of struggle I felt within me, one whose origins were mysterious but which — in ways I could only dimly understand — kept me shy, diminutive, unassertive. In other words, I didn't want to unwittingly foist upon my son the problems that had been foisted on me by parents and grandparents who did not care for introspection.

"Was there a particular moment when you first thought that therapy would be helpful?" the psychologist asked.

In fact, there had been such a moment — how had she known? — when I found myself having a silent tantrum in the soft corner of my son's day care center. Ben was eight months old; I was thirty years older and had just engaged a babysitter to stay with him for two afternoons a week so I could resume teaching freshman composition and writing at two local colleges. For an additional afternoon, I had enrolled him at an infant care center so that I could have three whole hours a week to myself for writing, relaxing, seeing friends.

Time alone! — a luxury in short supply following Ben's birth. To celebrate, one afternoon I had put on my running clothes: after spending the customary half hour with him as he acclimated himself to the center, I'd take a run in the park. But as if sensing my impatience, Ben began to wail inconsolably the moment I rose to leave. The other mothers filed out, casting me pitying looks. His teacher suggested that I stay a bit longer. So I sat down, frustrated and worried. Was something the matter with him? None of the other children cried when their mothers left.

Ben soon went back to his crawling, checking up on me only intermittently. From a distance he looked irresistible, vulnerable. Did I really want to leave him here? Maybe I should just take him home for the afternoon.

But I knew if I did that I'd find myself feeling trapped after about an hour. Why was it that on the verge of leaving my son I couldn't remember why I wanted to, yet in the midst of an endless day with him I was ravenous for time alone?

My reflections were interrupted after about fifteen minutes by Ben's teacher, who sidled over to me and said, "He seems fine now. Try leaving. But check back in a half hour or so."

Out I ran into the sunshine, down the block, and into the park. I took a long solitary run. It was early September, balmy and clear. On benches sat mothers tending their babies; a day ago I had been one of them, breast-feeding and watching the runners sweep by, envying them their freedom and self-absorption. But now that I was a runner, now that I was enjoying my first really free extended time in eight months, I found myself wanting to shout to these impassive women that I too had a child, that tomorrow I'd join their ranks again. Why did I feel so uncomfortable, so out of place, no matter where I was, even in this rejuvenating sun?

A long, circuitous route brought me back to the infant center. After a quick check on Ben, I'd be free to go home, take a hot bath, have a late, leisurely lunch, read my mail, the newspaper, make overdue phone calls. But greeting me in the lobby with a face full of tears was my son, thrashing about madly in the arms of his concerned teacher. "I think you'd better plan on staying," she said.

And that's how I found myself in the soft corner, sitting on cushions and pillows, surrounded by decals of Winnie-the-Pooh, watching toddlers drool into their training cups and have their diapers changed while the minutes of my freedom ticked by. I was the only mother there. Having ascertained that I was staying, my son steadfastly and triumphantly ignored me. "He feels so much better just to know you're here," his teacher said, as she put on a record, "Songs for Ones and Twos." I hated her. I knew she was right, absolutely right. To think of his physical welfare and emotional well-being was what I was paying her for, after all.

But who was thinking of mine?

Eight months of motherhood had exhausted me. I was living a

paradox: my son's birth was incontrovertible proof of my adult-hood, yet quite unaccountably I felt like a child myself, and more in need of mothering than I remembered ever feeling.

None of my close friends had children. My neediness es-tranged some of them and bewildered others. A few were sym-pathetic — those who weren't put off by how long it took me to return a phone call or by the capricious nature of a schedule that forced me to cancel plans at the last moment and freed me at odd hours when everyone who had a regular job was working. "Take time for yourself," they chorused, suggesting art or yoga classes. I had frequently offered such sensible advice to friends who suffered from too many demands placed on their time. But now I didn't want to be in a class; I didn't want to share a teacher or receive assignments. What I needed was a one-to-one tutorial.

Therapy offered the promise of a soothing drug I knew I re-sponded well to. For me therapy was not a concept or a process but the dream of a dimly lit, pleasant room to which I could retreat once a week to meet someone who would listen to me, who would be devoted to me, who would let me cry and would say comforting things. I had in fact been in therapy during my entire freshman year of college, and had subsequently sought out shorter-term professional counseling on several occasions. All of these experiences had been helpful. Yet as much as I longed to be in therapy, I was powerless to begin. Asking for referrals, making inquiries, placing phone calls, took time and energy, and that was exactly my predicament: I had neither.

I would probably have delayed indefinitely if my husband, David, a doctoral student in psychology, hadn't decided to seek therapy himself. Although I knew that one of the tacit require-ments of his therapeutic training was to undergo treatment, I was caught completely off guard when he announced one day that he had asked a colleague for a referral and had made an appointment.

What's *his* problem? I thought, unfairly, for I could see that Ben's arrival had confounded his life as profoundly as it had mine. We had been in the fifth year of an exceptionally close and happy marriage when our son was born. Our lives were not idyllic — we had sustained losses and hard times — but we managed to emerge from each crisis feeling more solidly devoted to each other.

Although we both wanted with equal fervor to have children, neither of us was prepared for Ben's assault on our time, energy, and intimacy. This was a new order of crisis, one we hadn't weathered before, and we couldn't reciprocally console and restore each other as we had in the past. In fact, we were hardly speaking.

Every day, watching David walk out the door to attend to his professional responsibilities, I felt abandoned and resentful of his freedom. Every night, David returned home resenting the fact that he had so many hats to wear and that his life was so fragmented. We'd talk in hurried sentences, for the baby would be crying; it would be time to go to sleep again, to apportion tasks for the next day when David would again feel stretched to breaking by the obligation to be student, professional, father, and husband, and I would again feel crushed by the weight of having to be mother and only mother.

I could sympathize with him from a distance. When he was at home, a touch away, I could think of only myself. That's why his impending therapy appointment goaded me into action. If he could have a regularly sanctioned excuse to leave the house and walk into a therapist's cozy office to talk about his problems with me and the baby, to escape for an hour each week from the family cauldron, then damn it, so could I.

None of this had appeared on my application form, I realized, catching my breath in the psychologist's office, wondering how in the world I had come to talk about David and my marriage. But this was exactly part of my problem: I felt out of control.

Until my son's birth I had been able to keep my feelings to myself — if I was angry at a friend, at my husband, at my mother,
they never had to know. Ben was different: he was a tiny know-
it-all. Implanted somewhere in his otherwise immature nervous
system was a perfectly tuned apparatus, which could detect the
slightest emotional changes in me. In his presence I feared for
my privacy: if I were angry or frustrated or excited about having
time away from him, as I had been that afternoon in day care,
he knew.

It was not only with him that I felt naked these days; it was
harder for me to quash my feelings in front of others, not because of any change in their ability to perceive me, but because
now I was too tired to do a good job of it. Devoting endless
hours to my son's care, I didn't have the stamina for the kind
of evasion, dishonesty, and emotional buck-passing I had been
engaged in until his arrival exhausted me. My duplicitous behavior had become too cumbersome, too uneconomical to continue. For the first time in my life, when my emotions came
calling at my front door, I didn't have the energy to drown out
the sound of their furious knocking.

The psychologist had been writing copiously as I spoke, but
hearing my voice tremble, she took off her glasses, and looked
at me fully for the first time. "This all must be very hard for
you," she said.

She spoke entirely without irony, a fact all the more remarkable because I had never heard the phrase "That must be very
hard for you" uttered so sincerely. She wasn't being sarcastic,
flip, or glib — *she meant it.* That this was one of the lines most
often parodied when people wanted to make fun of therapists
and therapy, that I had poked fun at this kind of comment myself, struck me as the only irony.

But this realization came later. All I registered at the moment
was that because of her caring I felt immense relief and grati-

tude. I hadn't even realized that I had been acting as if I were on a job interview, intent on impressing her with my general eligibility for admission to an exclusive, prestigious club, yet with one stroke she had both identified my anxiety and told me I needn't worry: she believed me. It was as if she had indicated a room with a bed and pillows, a room of unimaginable softness, and said, "There, you can rest for as long as you need to."

And I saw in that instant how different she was from anyone else in my life. When I complained to other people — parents, husband, friends, colleagues — they tried either to jolly me out of my mood or to tell me that I would feel better with a little more rest. Behind all of these exhortations was an implicit plea: please, oh please don't fall apart on us. Everyone needed me to carry on. But in this new room, so removed from my life, sat a stranger who simply said, "I hear what you're saying; it certainly sounds as if you are bearing a lot of burdens." This was an extraordinary gift.

When we were finished and she asked if I would prefer a man or a woman therapist, I said I had no preference, but later, at home, waiting to hear from the committee that met each month to match prospective clients with available therapists, I wished that I'd said, I would prefer you.

II

THREE WEEKS LATER, when I returned to the Institute for my
first appointment, an unfamiliar woman stepped into the waiting room to call my name. She was middle-aged, short, and had
light brown hair with a touch of gray, all of which reminded me
of my mother. She introduced herself as Dr. Marks, and led me
down a noisy corridor to an office next to a pay telephone. "This
won't be our regular room," she said. Then she asked why I
had sought treatment.

I recited my speech as if it were a piece in a play. She didn't
take notes — often she didn't even seem to be concentrating —
but she blinked her eyes with what I took to be fatigue. When
she consulted her clock, she did so, I thought, too obviously.
Assuming I'd either start crying or run out of time at any second, I delivered my voluminous monologue, describing what I
wanted out of therapy, at breakneck speed. Dr. Marks's version
of "you sound tired, it must be hard for you" was offered in the
middle of my explanation, and merely interrupted me. I finished with time to spare, and neither of us seemed particularly
moved. I, in fact, had never felt further from tears in my life.

Then I asked her if she had children. Of course she didn't. I
wondered how she would ever understand what I was talking
about. The possibility of finding with her the kind of comfort I
had experienced with the other therapist evaporated. Everything seemed hurried, insincere, perfunctory. She asked me a

few more questions and then, like football players milling about on the field, waiting for the clock to run down, we stared at each other until she said, "Our time is up."

I seriously thought about requesting a new therapist but decided to wait it out. Whether or not I liked Dr. Marks seemed beside the point. To undergo therapy, as I understood it, was akin to learning to operate a computer. If I were the glorified keypunch operator positioned at the keyboard, eager to type in all the data about myself, my past, dreams, and fears, then my therapist was both the central processing unit and printer, brilliantly incorporating all the raw data into something not only comprehensible but portable — a read-out that I could take home and study.

Implicit in this analogy was the notion that the tense that mattered most in therapy was the past. As a therapy client, all I was responsible for was a reconstructed account of my history which was as accurate as possible. The real time of the sessions — the forty-five minutes my therapist and I spent sitting and looking at each other — was for the express purpose of clarification: I'd be asked to elucidate, perhaps remember more vividly. Then the therapist would take my words and at some point, in some place — certainly not then and there — turn them into a kind of flowchart that would illustrate why I had turned out to be the person I was. To change myself I'd simply have to interrupt the usual patterns, initiate new ones, and — poof — I'd be transformed.

In this way, my therapist and I wouldn't really be working in tandem as much as in sequence: first I'd produce, then she would synthesize. Within the boundaries of such a static, scripted relationship I knew I could get along with Dr. Marks. Whatever had gone awry during the first week would be smoothed out by the next. My reservations about her were less important than how urgently I wanted help. And surely she could help me — after all, she was on the staff of a reputable training institute, wasn't she?

Yet at my next appointment I found myself distracted. We were in Dr. Marks's regular office, a small room on the quieter second floor of the Institute, with two chairs, an ottoman, and a couch. It was decorated with ceramic pieces, paintings, and dried flowers, and was lit by a soft, warm floor lamp. We sat diagonally across from each other, and both of us waited for me to say something. In the second before I began, I found myself staring at her coat. It hung on the back of the door, the only object in the room I could be sure belonged to her — an ugly jacket, part leather, part fake fur, in an unappealing orange color. I hated it.

And then there was the clock. Actually there were two, one on a table we both could see and one on a bookshelf that faced only her. They were electric, and I heard their drone underneath everything I said. What angered me was that Dr. Marks made no pretense of not looking at the clock, and seemed to do so more often as the session neared its end. Why couldn't she be more discreet? As a teacher, I knew how to keep track of the hour. In fact, a student once commended me on my ability to time a lesson perfectly without once consulting my watch. If I could master the art, why couldn't Dr. Marks? Why couldn't we at least pretend that our session wasn't premeasured, but rather a talk that just unfolded spontaneously? Was she too bored, or hungry, or tired to pay real attention to me? As if to rouse her, I began speaking more forcefully each time I saw her gaze drift.

Yet I seemed to be floundering. With everything to talk about, I could settle on nothing and heard myself talking very generally about how I was feeling, about events at work and at home. Even I was bored with what I was saying. Often she was silent, but occasionally she asked questions, usually about my previous experiences in therapy. In my confusion, I looked forward to those interruptions.

I told her that I had availed myself of psychological services three times: in college, in graduate school, and in the year before I became pregnant, but I wasn't even sure whether I should include the last time.

"Why not?" she demanded. She seemed to have a knack for selecting from my comments those details I considered either least significant or most distasteful.

Because, I explained, the therapist was a young female trainee, probably even younger than I was, at the medical clinic my husband and I had been using, and half the time I ended up talking as I would to a friend.

Dr. Marks asked what I meant. I told her about the time I had come to therapy after having fallen victim to an obscene phone call. The young woman paled listening to my story, and said, "I probably shouldn't do this," and proceeded to tell me that she had not only received a similar call, but had also been taken in by the man's scam. We ended up commiserating.

"How did that make you feel?" Dr. Marks asked, another stock question.

I hadn't thought about it before and I didn't want to think about it then. My job was to impart intelligence; analysis was her specialty, not mine.

"It sounds as if you had to take care of her," Dr. Marks said.

Suddenly I felt impatient, as if she were asking me to clarify something that needed no clarification. Everything had such huge implications in her office; even the tiniest event cast giant shadows and was overburdened with weighty importance. Couldn't anything be overlooked?

"How did the therapy end?" Dr. Marks asked.

I no longer felt relief when she asked me a question; at first it had helped structure the time, had rescued me from my fear of having nothing to say. But now her questions were becoming difficult.

I described how the therapy had ended. I'd walked into a session, and my therapist told me that this would be our last time together.

"How did you feel about that?" Dr. Marks asked.

"Well, I was upset," I said, "but it wasn't my therapist's fault; her supervisor had decided for her. Anyway, she'd helped me."

"Had you understood that this would only be a short-term commitment?" Dr. Marks asked, seizing, again, on the aspect of my story which I wanted least to examine.

"Yes, at first. But then she had led me to believe that because of the interesting nature of my case we could exceed the limited number of sessions."

"So when she suddenly had to terminate, what did this mean to you?"

I didn't know; I didn't care. I had been upset, of course, but at the time focusing on the anger didn't seem relevant. I wasn't denying that I had felt angry, but the anger had passed, leaving only a tiny scar, the scab at which Dr. Marks was now persistently picking.

"How did your therapy during college end?"

At last, an easy question. Therapy with that psychologist, a man, had ended in January of my sophomore year because I was transferring to a new school. This had been my most intensive experience with therapy, and it had been tremendously helpful for me. Yet almost as soon as I said this I remembered something I didn't want to. At my last session the doctor had propositioned me. I had panicked at first, sitting on his couch, twisting a strand of my hair around my finger, sweaty and tingly. But then I saw what was happening: he was testing my assertiveness, checking to see that what we had worked at so long and hard had sunk in. I relaxed some. But when I got up to leave, he hugged me and held me tightly. I couldn't break away when I wanted to. He was a huge, bearlike man, and for a moment I was afraid that he'd simply crush me.

Dr. Marks didn't say anything, though I assumed she had to be thinking the worst, so I hastened to assure her that however badly it ended, this doctor had helped me a great deal with many problems — boyfriend problems, love-life problems, mother problems.

"But how did that make you feel, to have him come on to you like that?" she asked.

I panicked. That was a question I had never asked myself. I had felt bewildered — nothing more. But of course I knew there was more. I had to defend him, for if I admitted how deeply he had betrayed me, then I couldn't believe that he had helped me. And he had — hadn't he?

"These experiences must color your perceptions of therapy now," she said.

But this didn't soothe me. Couldn't she give me credit for being able to separate out my different experiences? Why would I expect her to act as my other therapists had acted? Why did everything from our pasts have to have such enormous implications, cast such inescapable nets?

What a hole I was digging for myself. Of course the past is alive in the present — that's a cornerstone belief of psychotherapy which I shared; if I didn't, then I had absolutely no business there. But why was I acting as if I didn't? I considered myself an insightful, reflective person, at home with ambiguity and ambivalence, convinced in nothing so much as the power of articulation. And yet Dr. Marks's comments and questions had reduced me to someone who valued introspection not at all, someone who protested, "I know what I feel but I can't say it," someone lacking the patience to limn the nuances of her experience. How had I been maneuvered into defending such a patently indefensible position?

"I can promise you," Dr. Marks was saying, "that this treatment won't end until you are ready to end it." She sounded a bit overserious, as if she were intoning an oath. She was promising not to betray me, and I knew enough to remember that promise even though I wasn't yet sure I could believe her.

The sincerity in her tone allowed me to tell her of another, earlier experience in therapy which I had successfully buried until then, thinking that it wasn't really my experience. Nonetheless, I was a participant.

I was seventeen, in my senior year of high school. My brother, Ted, who was twelve, had developed a persistent numbness in one hand, which slowly traveled through his entire right side. He was referred by the pediatrician to a neurologist, whose tests revealed no organic problem. The neurologist recommended that my anxious parents take him to a psychologist.

My parents were mortified — psychological problems were not part of their vocabulary — but they made an appointment with a psychologist who, after brief interviews with each of us, decreed that the whole family had to show up Thursday evenings together. That meant gathering up my brother from his bed, for he wouldn't stir on his own, carrying him into the car, then out of it and into the therapist's office.

There we'd all watch my brother sit sullenly in his chair, not looking at anyone, not talking, not paying any attention to the therapist, who would be crooning softly, asking my brother to look him in the eye, to sit back in his chair, to draw a house, a tree, a person. And suddenly, in reaction to what seemed a perfectly innocuous statement or request from the therapist, my brother would snap, unleashing a fit of temper no one in my family had ever seen, or probably even imagined. Transformed into an alien creature, he would hit, smash, bite, curse, throw objects, scream, as if possessed.

Although he was the sole target of these outbursts, the psychologist remained infuriatingly calm; even in the midst of a direct assault, he retained the air of a conjurer, a dramatist who actually enjoyed staging these tantrums, who either didn't notice or didn't care that my brother's skin was sizzling with fury, or that my parents and I were overcome with emotion we couldn't begin to label or understand. I recognized that the performance was in some way intended for the family's benefit as well as my brother's but couldn't see how or why.

Several times the therapist tried to get us to talk about how we felt watching my brother act this way, but it was like asking us to converse in a foreign language. None of us was equipped to watch such a performance, let alone figure out what we felt about it. To me such questions — the entire operation, in fact — seemed torturous and sadistic; I hated the psychologist, dreaded coming. Why won't he leave us all alone? I'd cry to myself. Nothing positive seemed to issue from the sessions — after the hour on Thursday nights my brother was shoveled back in the car and into bed. I don't know what he did all week, but I'm sure the rest of us tried to forget about what we had seen.

After about two months of sessions, however, my brother's numbness mysteriously receded. He not only returned to school but also began attending therapy sessions by himself, the family having been summarily dismissed.

"The shrink blew it, though," I told Dr. Marks. "He succeeded in allowing my brother to vent his anger, but in the process he made my brother so furious at him that he couldn't confide in the doctor once the anger was spent. He only went for about a month on his own, and then refused to go again."

Dr. Marks asked if my family had changed after this experience. We hadn't. We never even spoke about it. I had always assumed that my parents finally understood my brother's cure as a kind of secular exorcism. But now I rejected this analogy. The demons that plagued my brother hadn't come from without and weren't banished into oblivion, but were nurtured within him, within us all. If anything had summoned them, it was my family's persistent denial of their existence.

Dr. Marks didn't immediately comment. I had always cried profusely through my brother's therapy sessions and was close to tears again now. Could it be that after all these years I was still angry at his therapist, remembering the enjoyment he seemed to derive from seeing my family squirm? Or was I realizing for the first time that to focus exclusively on my distaste for the therapist was to miss the point? My brother had gone on a remarkable journey in that little office, a journey by himself, a journey no one else in the family could accompany him on — beyond words, beyond reason — as if the circuitry of rational thinking had shorted out. No one in my family had ever traveled that far; in fact, we had all worked hard to deny that such a trip need ever be taken.

"You sound as if you're a bit envious," Dr. Marks said.

I was incredulous. Envious of what?

"Your brother's journey. His anger. His therapist."

That was ridiculous. I didn't want a therapist like him. I wanted to love my therapist. Why was she making this so hard for me? If only she were less detached; if only she were more discreet; if only she had better taste in clothes. Imagine, I thought, anyone spending good money on a jacket as ugly as the one hanging on her door.

III

THE MORNING of my next appointment Ben woke up before five, moaning softly in his crib. Although he didn't feel feverish, he refused his bottle and couldn't be comforted. David, dressing for work, asked me if I wanted him to stay home, but I knew he expected me to say no. He left at seven. After an hour of rocking Ben and putting him in the infant swing, both of which usually soothed him, I called the pediatrician, who told me to come in at one that afternoon, five hours away.

Ben moaned and cried without stop. Even when he dozed off for a few whimpering, fitful minutes, he seemed less asleep than semicomatose. Picking him up from his crib after one such spell, I noticed that fluid was oozing from his ear. Of all the times since Ben's birth that I had phoned the doctor, this time I was the most out of control. The doctor agreed that I should come in right away.

Hysterical, as if I had just received a dread diagnosis, I bundled Ben up and ran downstairs to flag a taxi. In my arms Ben felt limp, beyond crying, beyond sleep, utterly beyond my reach.

An ear infection, the doctor told me, after an infuriatingly long wait. A punctured eardrum. He prescribed an antibiotic. "That's all?" I said. "He looks so listless."

"I've seen much worse," the doctor said, smiling.

Within an hour of taking the first dose of the bubble-gum pink medicine, Ben had settled down for a calm nap. Relieved and exhausted, I too climbed into bed, and in the minutes before sleep I found myself thinking about my brother, Ted, who had been on my mind more in the past months since Ben's birth than he had been in my entire life.

Ted had generously offered to come stay with us after Ben was born, to help us out around the house in whatever capacity he could. His thoughtfulness touched me; I hadn't expected it, and frankly never thought I'd have to take him up on it.

But David and I had underestimated the topsy-turvy effect of a newborn on a household. The second day Ben was at home with us, he cried all afternoon and night. David and I took turns walking and rocking him. At three in the morning I found myself in the living room with a child both hiccoughing and shrieking. None of the lullabies I had so carefully learned was soothing. Nursing calmed him only for the short time that my nipple was in his mouth; if it slipped out, the crying began again. Sick of shifting him from arm to arm, sick from fatigue and strain, I held my son out in front of me as if he were a garment I was debating whether to buy or not, and I shook him, knowing in the instant that I did that it was a futile gesture, that it would stop neither his crying nor his hiccoughs; worse, that I would regret it instantly, and feel like a monster for losing my temper.

I knew also that it wasn't only my son's cries that I was trying to staunch.

The next morning, in tears, I called Ted at medical school in Philadelphia. "Do you want me to come for the weekend?" he asked. "I can be on the next plane."

I couldn't speak. If he had said, "I'm coming," I wouldn't have argued. Instead, he asked what I wanted. And I was dumbstruck.

"Talk to me, Roberta," he said. "Tell me. I'm your *brother*, for God's sake."

As if that was supposed to clarify my predicament. For me, his calling attention to our relationship simply fogged the issue. Yes, he was my brother and what did that mean? What had it ever meant? To him, it apparently meant that I could speak the truth. To me it offered no such refuge. I honestly couldn't say, in those seconds that I clutched the phone, if I didn't know what I really wanted, or if I knew and couldn't say.

Part of what I wanted, of course, was not to be asked what I wanted. I wanted Ted to relieve me of the burden of having to admit that I wanted anything, that I needed someone or something.

If he hadn't threatened to hang up and call back when I was more communicative I wouldn't have spoken at all. But facing this threat I stammered yes, if he could come I'd appreciate it.

He was a great help and comfort. I remember one particular morning when, desperate for a bath, I marched Ben around the apartment for what felt like miles in a futile effort to get him to nap. Ted, who had been cleaning up the breakfast dishes, must have sensed my frustration through the wall, for though I said nothing aloud he suddenly materialized and plucked the cranky baby from my arms. I was immobilized with relief and chagrin. "Go," he said, and like a good child I obeyed. I drew my bath and climbed in. From the living room, in the gentlest tones imaginable, as if he were reading a delightful fairy tale, I heard Ted's voice reciting to Ben the names of the nerves in the face and the bones of the spine, the hand, the leg. Ben was quiet. I soaked.

"I didn't know you had it in you," I told Ted after I was dressed.

"At least one of us does," he said. We stared at each other, daring each other to continue. We often found ourselves in such a standoff, trading flippancies instead of speaking our minds. What I meant to say was thank you; what he wanted to say was you're welcome. But the old patterns of our conversation over-whelmed us. Anyway, I was angry — angry that he had been able to calm my son when I hadn't, angry because I had seen a side of him I hadn't known about.

"He's a little complainer," my grandmother used to say of her youngest grandson. "He didn't get his shipment of smiles to-day," my parents would say as we snuggled in bed together on a weekend morning and watched Ted frown. No one could make him happy.

He was a moody child, quick to take offense. He claims this was justified, that he had to claw his way to be noticed, and that I subjected him to the torture only a jealous older sibling can inflict. When we played dress-up with my older friends I in-sisted that he be a girl. Or a slave. I made him fetch things for me. He has countless horror stories, which I can't stand to hear and which he relishes.

He fought dirty, and would often bring me to tears. "They shouldn't fight like that," my grandmother would say during a car trip when Ted and I mercilessly teased each other, when we bickered during games, when we shouted at each other over dinner. "You're brother and sister," she'd say, as if our argu-ments were unnatural, shameful, as if there were something ter-ribly wrong with us.

In fact, we liked butting heads, putting our hands all over each other: we loved each other, in our own combative, perhaps unorthodox way. That was a truth both of us were too young to voice and which eluded our elders. Our physicality, our giddi-ness, enabled us to express both the closeness and the resent-ment we felt toward each other. Rarely were we allowed the op-portunity. "You're laughing now," the adults around us would warn, "but soon you'll be crying."

Crying. Though I don't recall the sound of his cry, that is what I think of when I think of my little brother. Maybe Ted hadn't been an unusually unhappy baby — I know now that my parents tend to exaggerate, especially things that they perceive as negative. Maybe he had simply gone about his business, alerting his family to his needs in the only way he could. In truth, I remember astonishingly little about his early life. He arrived when I was a few months past my fifth birthday and old enough to have clearer memories than I do. But I can't remember my mother being pregnant or my parents discussing with me the fact that I would soon have a sister or brother. I don't remember my mother leaving and my grandmother coming to stay. Had we indeed talked, and had I blocked it out along with everything else? Did I bridle at their explicit expectation that I would now be the "big sister," full of love and understanding and sacrifice? Was my total amnesia the result of an underground volcano of rage?

For I can't picture the infant Ted anywhere in our house. I can see the changing table on which my mother had lined up ointments, salves, and jars of Q-Tips and cotton balls, but I don't recall where his crib was placed, or that one afternoon I pummeled him out of a nap. My mother found me. She said she hit me, screamed at me. I have to take her word for it.

My clearest memories of Ted's arrival are the earliest ones. I remember, for instance, that when my mother came home from the hospital she had to stay in bed for about a week because of an infection. A nurse, a skinny woman in white with a pinched face and long red fingers, slept over and tended the baby. Sometimes she took me downstairs to the park. One afternoon I began throwing rocks into the street. A white car passed by after the rock had left my hand, and the rock struck it. The car circled the block and returned. The driver, a husky, scowling man, threw open his door. In an instant the nurse gathered me up as if I were a pile of laundry and carried me upstairs. I heard her whispering to my mother. Was I punished? Talked to?

Even before this memory is another: I am wearing a blue

pleated skirt and white blouse and a pastel blue spring coat, although I don't recall who dressed me. I'm standing in a park across the street from the hospital. Could my father have left me alone to go upstairs to see them — his wife and newborn son? It seems impossible, but I have a clear image of the moment my father warned me that I mustn't budge or speak while he was away. And then my father is back, and he kneels beside me on one knee and tells me to count up so many floors to the one where I'll see my mother standing at a window. "Look, she's waving!" he says. But I don't see her move; I hardly see her at all. "Blow her a kiss," my father exhorts, and so I do.

Then there is a car ride. My mother, a nurse, and my baby brother and I are all sitting in the back seat. (We wouldn't all fit, of course, and my father wouldn't be driving alone, up front.) Eagerly I ask to hold the baby. As soon as he's in my arms he cries. I want to chuck him out of the car. But we are going underground, into a long tunnel, and we can't change lanes or open the windows, and everything is suddenly dark.

The doorbell woke us up — Ben and I had both slept the afternoon away. It was my running partner with a bag of take-out from the local Chinese restaurant. Over Ben's cries I told her that I'd never been happier to see anyone, that this had been the kind of day that makes mothers crazy.

"Ben has a wonderfully expressive cry," she said, taking him from me, listening, studying his red and wrinkled face. "Remember, it's all he can do now, the only way he can express himself."

I'd never thought of it that way. For all the endless speculation my family had engaged in on the meaning of Ted's cries, this was one explanation we had never considered.

I thanked her for this new perspective and tried to hold onto it after she left. But during his bath, when Ben wailed as he always did, I realized I was still a child of my parents who

couldn't stand to hear a baby cry — so much raw emotion —
who couldn't construe an alternate interpretation for crying save
inconsolable misery.

By seven that evening, when David returned home so that I
could keep my appointment with Dr. Marks, Ben was the calm-
est he'd been in fourteen hours — so calm that I wondered if
David even believed my harrowing account of the day. "Give
Ben his medication before you leave," he said.

"Can't you?" I asked. I was running late. He didn't answer.
As I stood in the kitchen, measuring out the viscous liquid, I
suddenly remembered that Ted had been susceptible to ear in-
fections as an infant. On his dressing table there had been a
purple vial with a glass dropper containing an oily fluid, which
my mother put in his ear on those days he cried himself into a
stupor, as Ben had that morning, cries that snaked into my ear
and couldn't be stopped, cries that made me want to cry. But I
couldn't, for I was the mother, the adult, the big sister. Babies —
my brother, my son — cry with impunity. No matter how much
I long to, I cannot; and I feel, however irrationally, that I never
have been able to, even when the baby was me.

IV

EACH WEEK at the end of my session, even before I had time to completely close the door behind me, Dr. Marks's next patient, a young woman dressed in black with long black hair, would sweep by me into the office. She reminded me of a bird of prey.

I never mentioned this woman during my sessions; the annoyance the sight of her aroused in me, so pronounced each time I left, abated by the time I returned. But one evening I found her sitting on the floor outside Dr. Marks's office as I walked in for the *start* of my session. This was carrying eagerness a bit too far.

Why couldn't she wait downstairs like everyone else, I asked myself, my indignation no less acute for being unvoiced. The woman so distracted me that I didn't know how to begin the session. Dr. Marks seemed completely at ease in the silence, smiling at me in a way that neither encouraged nor reproached, but simply marked time.

I had arrived having rehearsed my first remarks, much as chess players plan their opening gambit, yet the image of this woman had invaded my mind and would not be quashed. As pervasive as static, she interfered with my thoughts. Was she hovering outside the door even now, listening in, wishing me gone, dead, finished? That I might be reacting to the desperation she couldn't or didn't care to disguise never occurred to me; all I could identify at the time was her indiscretion, her inability to wait or to observe a basic, unwritten tenet of psychothera-peutic etiquette. Almost against my will, I finally said, "That woman is always right outside when I leave," hoping Dr. Marks would infer that her presence merely amused me, or piqued my curiosity.

"Yes," Dr. Marks said, waiting for me to go on. Instantly I regretted having said anything. What would I go on to say now?

"I guess I don't like thinking about your other clients," I said, aware even as I spoke how ridiculous I sounded. Of course she had other clients — that was the nature of her work — but until that moment I don't think I had understood what this meant: Dr. Marks listened to other people besides me. Some of these people had far worse problems than I had; this I knew, having learned through one of my husband's colleagues that Dr. Marks specialized in working with adult children of alcoholic parents. The woman lurking outside the door could easily have had such a history, could have been someone with real problems, for whom daily survival was a torment. "She's probably much more interesting a case than I am," I said. I couldn't look at Dr. Marks as I spoke, making my voice so small I could hardly hear it.

"What if she is?" Dr. Marks asked, as if she didn't realize the painful nature of her question. Suddenly, I couldn't even re-member why I had come. My problems seemed negligible, in-effable, elusive, insignificant, fleeting twinges that haunted me but had no real form.

"Why aren't your problems enough for you?" Dr. Marks asked.

"They're enough for me," I replied, "but I worry that they're not enough for you. That I'm boring you."

Oh no, Dr. Marks could have said then. You're the most in-sightful person I've ever worked with. I couldn't possibly be bored with you. You're my most intriguing case, my best client.

Or, she could have said, Well, to tell the truth, they are a bit mundane, don't you think? Let's try to hurry along so I can

devote my office time to people who really need me, like that
poor woman you've noticed, and then let's have dinner, let's go
to the movies, let's be friends.

Either would have been fine; which I would have preferred,
I wasn't entirely sure.

Instead, Dr. Marks said, "Your problems are special because
they're yours," stressing "yours." Mine.

This certainly wasn't what I'd hoped she would say, but I
recognized nonetheless that she was making an important
point; that she was offering me a kind of lifeline I could latch on
to, and I did, trusting that my being saved wasn't necessarily
contingent on understanding the mechanics of my rescue.

Yet I felt vaguely dissatisfied. Was Dr. Marks not that skilled
a therapist? Or was I simply not the kind of patient I had expected to be? If anyone had asked me two months earlier to
describe myself as a therapy client, I would have painted the
picture of a woman whose entire week was structured around
the therapy session, who looked forward unhesitantly to each
session, who hated to leave, who hungered to come again, who
had automatically bonded with her therapist. In short, I would
have imagined myself the dark-haired woman waiting outside
the door. Yet here I was, despising the woman who was playing
the role written for me, and not knowing why. Two months into
therapy, I still had no feeling about my therapist; I didn't love
her, I didn't trust her. Worst of all, she didn't love me.

All of this was remarkable news. For as long as I had been
aware of myself as a social person, I had believed in my ability
to trust others, to form deep attachments to people, to give and
receive love easily, to need others and feel needed by them. To
question this seemed unthinkable. If I wasn't yet involved with
Dr. Marks, it was because she was an unapproachable person.
Even the woman who interviewed me when I first came to the
Institute showed more human warmth than Dr. Marks did.
What I meant by this was that the other psychologist had re-

sponded to me. Most people responded to me; only Dr. Marks seemed inexplicably, perversely aloof. For I was the perfect patient: I was punctual, knew when my time was up, spoke deferentially and thoughtfully, displayed an impressive understanding of psychology for a layperson, and paid my bills on time.

Dr. Marks didn't seem to notice. I didn't expect her to tell me straight out that I was the most engaging client she had ever had the pleasure of working with, but she could have looked as if such a comparison were on her mind. If she in fact preferred the kind of patient who was less composed and considerate, a patient like the woman outside the door, she could have told me that, too. I was very adaptable and perceptive, my antennae finely tuned to other people's reactions to me; I would have picked up her most circumspect signal and accepted it as subtly as she had transmitted it.

Such a sign never came. Sometimes I could elicit a guffaw; that was all. She refused to be seduced. Of course, if I had succeeded in charming her, I would have then demeaned her, as I secretly did most people who professed to care for me. For precisely this reason she had to withhold what I most wanted from her. My frustration grew. She leaned back in her chair, impenetrably calm, put her feet up on the ottoman we shared, took a lazy look at her clock, and gave me all the time in the world to be me. Whoever that was.

Finding out who I was entailed a confession of sins. No one could know me, I assumed, until she knew my darkest side. You may not believe this, Dr. Marks, but in college I was a bit of a kleptomaniac; I lifted clothing and jewelry from stores, from people's rooms. To this day I'd often rather lie than tell the truth; I am an envious person, a jealous person, a hypocrite — for example, although I am a professed nonsmoker who insists on being served in the nonsmoking sections of restaurants and

planes and demands that visitors not smoke in my home, I occasionally crave a cigarette, a craving I can neither squelch nor
fathom. As infrequently as once every few months I either bum
a cigarette or buy a pack, stow it in an inner compartment of my
purse and smoke furtively, as a reformed alcoholic might sneak
a drink.

I didn't know what kind of reaction to expect. Dr. Marks had
the requisite No Smoking signs in her office. That she would
lash into me seemed improbable, but when she didn't, when
she merely asked what associations cigarettes had for me, I felt
incredibly relieved. Relishing the memories I began relating to
her, I told her about my first week of college, when my room-
mate and I, dizzy with our freedom, bought our first pack together, smoking in the student lounge, in the cafeteria, like real
grown-ups.

"You have fond memories of that time," Dr. Marks observed.

"But smoking is such a noxious habit."

"A cigarette once every few months hardly sounds like a
habit," she said. "It sounds to me as if you give yourself a hard
time for wanting to indulge in a little nostalgia, for wanting to
step out, to have fun."

No one defines smoking as *fun*, I countered silently. But she
had put it this way only because I had; according to my own
memories, within my own context, smoking a cigarette once in
a very great while was fun, and nothing more.

I left therapy that day in excellent spirits. Finally I had something, however intangible, to take home with me. It wasn't just
her conclusion that mattered, but the course of the entire conversation, as if it were a Chinese puzzle box and each step taken
toward the innermost compartment was intrinsically satisfying.
I wished the conversation had been on tape.

It wasn't until I was down in the lobby of the Institute, stopping at the desk to pay my bill, that I realized that I had not
seen the dark-haired woman upon leaving.

Just then, I glanced up. Dr. Marks was coming down the stairs wearing her orange coat. She must have put it on the moment I left her office. This gave me angry pause. If she left so quickly after seeing me, how would she remember everything I had told her? Wasn't she supposed to write it all down, to keep progress notes? Didn't I merit thoughtful musings in the solitude of her office? Did she think I was talking to myself?

We ended up at the same corner, each hoping to hail a cab in the windy twilight. In a way it was my fantasy come true: here we were, face to face, out on the street, out of the bounds of her office and that increasingly peculiar one-sided relationship.

She was the first to initiate small talk, something about the scarcity of cabs. One finally stopped and she got in. Her head was barely visible over the back of the seat; it was as if the cab had swallowed her. Who is she? I wondered, watching the cab disappear downtown into the darkness, and how did she manage to affect me in such confusing ways? She seemed as stubbornly absent from my life as she was present in it; or was it simply that she figured in my life, and I didn't in hers?

V

I am in a reception room in the Institute. Dr. Marks and I are having a session. Gradually, her colleagues drift into the room and begin to greet her, ask her questions, ask her advice, consult with her. She obliges, hesitantly at first, but soon asks if I would mind waiting outside for a moment. The scene shifts to my ninth grade biology lab. I am working on an experiment at the desk in the front of the room when overhead there is a tremendous sound, and bursting through the wall above me is an enormous creature, part fish, part sea slug, only barely alive. It flops helplessly on the lab table and we must save its life.

"What do you think the dream is about?" Dr. Marks asked me. I had no idea; I was simply thrilled to have dreamt it, to be able to tote it to therapy as proof of my devotion. I supposed it was about wanting to have her to myself, I volunteered.

She asked me if I felt safe at therapy.

"Yes," I said.

"Even with dead whales crashing into the room?"

I flushed, panicked. I hadn't thought of it that way. I hadn't analyzed the dream at all.

"It doesn't have to mean that," I said, defensively. Her analysis had taken only a second. She was being careless, irresponsible. "It could mean something else. You could be wrong."

"What if I am?" she asked, and her question set my head reeling. She wasn't supposed to make mistakes — she was supposed to have the answers.

The dream had thrust us — me — out of the past tense and into the present, which had come crashing through the wall, demanding immediate attention. What I could recall about my past and my commentary on it were much less important than the fact that Dr. Marks and I were two people sitting in a room talking to each other, reading each other's nonverbal language, shifting in our seats, musing, scheming, dreaming. Maybe she didn't know all the answers; maybe I wasn't at a computer terminal at all. But if that was the case, then where the hell was I?

What a dangerous gift I ended up bringing — one that turned on the giver, revealing something about me of which I had not been aware but couldn't deny. And I felt embarrassed that I had tried to deny what my unconscious had so patently given away. What else had I unwittingly said or done that had rendered me transparent to Dr. Marks's eyes? Even the most innocuous statements could be fraught with meaning. I felt suddenly as if I were oozing secrets about myself.

One night Dr. Marks asked if I was aware that I was financially responsible for sessions that I had to cancel, alluding to a recent session I had to miss because of illness. She asked if I was angry about this policy; when I assured her I wasn't, she asked why, then, I hadn't yet paid for the missed session.

In fact I had; a bookkeeping error was subsequently uncovered and rectified. But for the moment, sitting in her office, I froze. That Dr. Marks had thought for even one moment that I hadn't paid my bill mortified me. I explained at great length my innocence, only to have her ask me, again and again, if I was angry about the incident, angry at her assumption, angry at her.

Or was I angry about something else? For example, that three weeks had lapsed between my initial intake interview and subsequent start of therapy? Or that I hadn't been able to arrange to have therapy sessions on the day or at the time I preferred?

All her questions I wanted to swat away; they were beside the point. Anger wasn't the problem as much as convincing Dr. Marks of several facts: I wasn't the kind of person who expected something for nothing or complained about the rules; I understood that institutions had to set policy. No, I wasn't angry, not at all. Yet she stubbornly persisted. Was I angry that my husband's therapy had begun two weeks before mine had and that he could have his at a more convenient hour?

NO, I screamed inwardly, NO. Aren't we ever going to get off the subject of whether or not I'm angry? I never stopped to think that she might repeat her questions for any other reason than to annoy me. I believed I wasn't secretly angry.

In truth, the list of things that angered me went on for pages and pages — that was the main reason I had to deny my anger — and worst of all, everything that riled me was ridiculous. Sure, I was angry about having to pay for a session I missed, but how could I justify that? How could I explain that what angered me most was that Dr. Marks wasn't a mind reader? *She* angered me. How come you still look at the clock during our sessions? I cried at her when I was by myself; how can you have such lousy taste in clothes; how can you be so detached, so cruel, so uninvolved, how can you be so wrong about me, *how can you not love me?*

A few weeks later, in mid-December, I had to cancel a second therapy session in order to consult with a surgeon who was scheduled to operate on me during Christmas vacation. The surgery itself was minor; missing a second therapy session in a month was not. I felt compelled to explain over and over why I had to miss the session, as if my explanations would form a barrier protecting me from the verbal blows and accusations I imagined Dr. Marks would hurl at me: Admit it, you're not really involved in this treatment, are you?

When she failed to make any such statement, I felt on even

shakier ground. The more she seemed to trust me, the greater the tide of excuses pouring out of me.

"Why do you think I don't believe you?" she asked.

"I'm afraid you'll mistakenly assume something that isn't true about me," I confessed.

"What if I do?" Questions like that left me feeling as if my feet were no longer on the floor. "Couldn't you change my mind?" she added.

My torrent of words *was* offered in the hope of changing her mind, yet I realized, as she asked her last question, that I despaired of this ever coming to pass. I feared that her picture of me was immutable. In fact, I had been assuming that she was incapable of changing her mind, and didn't put much stock in my words even as I uttered them.

"Are you frightened about the surgery?" she asked gently. Once again I felt a reflexive NO rising in my throat — didn't this woman ever quit? — but stopped.

I said I wasn't, explaining the procedure to repair an inguinal hernia to her as graphically as it had been explained to me, stressing how minor it would be. I'd even be receiving a local anaesthetic, so I would be awake in the operating room, and I'd be able to come home after a day or two. She listened patiently. She must have seen that I was beginning to have the faintest inkling, finally, that my recitation was not really the answer to the question she had posed.

VI

"You're in therapy?" Denise asked. My mothers' group
had just ended, and five of us were trying to grab a quick lunch
in a new French café, the only restaurant in our neighborhood
wide enough to accommodate baby strollers, before our children
woke up.

I couldn't read her reaction. Was she offended that I hadn't
shared this news with the group earlier? Or did she not approve
of therapy? Maybe I should have trusted my initial hesitancy.
Yet these women knew just about everything else about me. I
felt obliged to let them know.

"I wish I could afford to go," said Ann, whose spacious apartment we had just left, and who had never before intimated that
she had any financial problems.

"I wish I could afford the *time*," said Judy, whose husband
attended a poker game twice weekly.

"I go at night," I explained, "when David is home."

"I never liked therapy at night," Denise said. "I always had
nightmares."

"Oh, I liked going at night," said Martha, dreamily. "It's
worse when you have to squeeze in a session during the day
and then have to rush off to work and you never have time to
digest what happened."

The conversation was spirited, and included everyone but

me. I stared at the handwritten menu, amazed that every woman at the table had once been in therapy herself. Yet why, as I listened to them, did I feel left out?

We were an unlikely group — five professional women on maternity leaves of varying lengths, five strangers thrown together by a parent resource organization, a kind of computer dating service for women with kids, because we happened to live within a few blocks of each other and have children who were close in age. Yet, after six months, I felt closer to them than I did to some friends I had known and loved for twenty years; closer, at times, it seemed, than I felt to David.

We took turns hosting the meetings. Each week we settled our children on blankets on the floor, and bitched: about our husbands who were part of the problem instead of part of the solution; about our childless friends who didn't understand that simply going back to work wasn't the cure-all; about our mothers who insisted our babies would starve if we didn't immediately start giving them solid food instead of breast milk; about our pediatricians who wanted us to let our children cry themselves to sleep; about bus drivers who made us fold up our strollers before boarding; and about waiters, like the one coming toward us, unable to mask his distaste at having to gingerly pick his way around the tangle of strollers and overstuffed diaper bags in order to serve us our quiches and salads. He looked as if he wished he could have flung the food in our faces, and the hell with his tip.

We must have seemed so archetypically *female*, I thought, housewives on an extended coffee klatch, earth mothers with our milk-stained blouses and full bodies; and yet I couldn't help but think of us as a group of army buddies at a veterans' reunion. The experience we had undergone together — bearing children — was antithetical to combat but no less intense, and we couldn't evoke it except in each other's company. Together we would cry from laughing, not knowing what else to do, tears that made me shiver with the stunning realization that someone else was fighting the same battles I was.

I needed this camaraderie as much as I had ever needed anything in my life. Yet, for all the soul-bearing secrets that the group tolerated, it forbade one thing: change. We had tacitly agreed to see ourselves as victims — of our families, our society, ourselves. And any time someone suggested a way that our victimization could be quietly but assertively overcome, the suggestion was dismissed — too expensive, time-consuming, impractical, indulgent, strenuous, impossible.

"You're lucky," Denise said to me, the conversation having circled back to the confession that had launched it, and the other women nodded, as if luck had anything to do with the way I'd had to claw through the inertia that had beset me. The time and money were not easy to come by, I wanted to shout; even the Institute's modest sliding scale fee strained our budget. And finding the time took nights of hard negotiation with David.

But what Denise really meant was, "You're different."

Maybe that's why I felt left out: was it possible, I wondered, that therapy had already begun to change me? Instead of waiting for the extra money to fall into my lap or for a babysitter to volunteer herself, I had simply managed to finagle, within the severe limits on my time and finances, enough of both to afford me a weekly visit to a therapist. "I want to" was my only justification. And this assertion seemed to have weakened my bond to the mothers' group, tied together as we had been by a vow of resignation.

I had listened to them week after week. I knew the extent of their unhappiness, their bewilderment, their frustration. "You must at least *think* of seeing someone," I finally said to the group at large.

"I have my old shrink's number posted on my refrigerator," said Martha sadly, "right next to the number of the pediatrician. But somehow I never get to call."

*

While we were eating, a man walked into the café whom I recognized. John and I had been in the same graduate program seven years before. At least ten years older than the rest of us, he had arrived with an impressive portfolio of publications which we all envied. Over the years I heard how his reputation had grown, but he and I had lost touch with each other. In fact, though we lived in the same neighborhood, this was the first time I had seen him since I had finished the program.

From an overstuffed leather briefcase he extracted a manila folder, and from it a pile of messy, handwritten papers. He ordered a cappuccino and uncapped his fountain pen. He put on his eyeglasses only to push them, a moment later, to his forehead, so he could sigh loudly and rub his eyes. When he pulled off his beret I was stunned to see that his hair was gray.

Once we had been colleagues; we had taken coffee breaks together during our seminars, critiqued each other's papers, helped each other in the library. Now it was as if I were invisible. Even if he had glanced at my table he wouldn't have seen me; *I* couldn't see me. I felt submerged in the knot of strollers and babies, in the resigned voices of my friends, in the dirty dishes waiting to be collected. John and I had become caricatures of ourselves: the successful academic and the harried mother.

Except I wasn't only a mother. In fact, in five minutes I'd have to excuse myself and rush home with Ben, hoping to find the babysitter waiting for us. In a flash I'd change into a skirt and blouse and catch the bus to work. I too had papers to grade. And I had to remember to ask the babysitter if she could come Saturday night, so David and I could go out for dinner. For I was also a wife, at least one night a week.

When I stood up, Denise said she'd leave with me. At the door we nearly ran into a woman who was dashing into the café. She was meeting John, I suspected. Sure enough, from outside, I saw her rush up to his table. They kissed, and from his briefcase he withdrew a rose, which he placed on the placemat in front of her.

Denise and I lumbered uptown. She asked if the conversation in the café had upset me. It seemed easiest to say no. "It's just that you seem so well adjusted," she said, sounding slightly exasperated. "I mean, you're back at work, you have a regular babysitter, you have a life with David. You seem like the last person to need therapy."

Was this a compliment or a commentary on my self-indulgence? Was there a waiting list? Had I cut in line? I felt provoked in so many ways I couldn't begin to sort out my reactions. We walked silently for a while. "Did you notice that man in the corner of the café, the one sitting by himself, with the beret?" I asked. Denise nodded. "I went to graduate school with him."

She stared at me. "Why didn't you say hello?"

I shrugged. It had to do with not feeling so well adjusted.

VII

ONE EVENING, not long after I told Dr. Marks about my surgery, I came to therapy unhappy because I had found out that two women from my mothers' group had made dinner plans without me. Dr. Marks encouraged me to speak for several minutes about my sense of being shut out, and then gently said, "The way you sound reminds me of a dream you had." She went on to recall a scene from a dream I had told her about a few weeks before in which I saw my mother from the back.

It hadn't been a particularly emotional moment in the original dream, but juxtaposed here, at this juncture, I felt my throat tighten with suppressed tears. "Do you feel as if your mother's back is turned to you?" she asked, and suddenly I found myself weeping. The sadness was more profound than any I had ever experienced. It came from a source I couldn't pinpoint but which extended inward, downward, as if from a chamber in my heart I wouldn't have known about if Dr. Marks hadn't found it for me by simply placing an image from one of my dreams in the context of our conversation. Her work seemed almost physical, or rather spatial, in the same way that a child learns to solve jigsaw puzzles by first turning all the pieces right-side up, and then placing like pieces together — only the pieces here were feelings, one that was current and one very much older, which belonged together.

I had nothing to say; there was nothing left but the feeling of abandonment. For the first time in therapy I was not only script-less but also defenseless, unable to pretend I wasn't devastated, no longer needing to understand why I felt this way but simply feeling. I wasn't compelled to explain that in reality my mother never abandoned me. I could simply sit there and feel bad. Even Dr. Marks's silence didn't feel awkward. Crying in front of her wasn't as difficult as it had seemed in the abstract; the fact that she was sitting there watching me, which had always prevented me from giving in to tears before, faded from prominence. She made no move to comfort me, but neither did she try to stop me. When I lifted my gaze and dabbed at my eyes with a tissue she met me with a look that seemed to say, "I'm here — you're here," riveting my attention as if she had taken my chin in her hand as she would a child's.

I had another dream the week of our last session before winter vacation: The surgeon was performing the operation on me and I was awake, feeling no pain, and worried that he could see what was inside me and I couldn't. I was desperate for the equivalent of makeup for internal organs.

"Are you afraid of the procedure?" Dr. Marks asked, for what seemed like the millionth time. But this time I reacted differently. Instead of raging, even silently to myself, I began to think about the question. Something was scary to me, even if I wasn't sure what it was.

Slowly, it dawned on me that she asked the same question over and over again not because she didn't know she was re-peating herself, or because she had forgotten the answer, but because she was hoping that maybe this time I would actually answer it, not deflect or evade it. In other words, she was sta-tionary, but I was somehow moving, and the best way to gauge my movement was in relation to how far I'd traveled since the last time she asked me, Are you angry? Are you scared?

"In the dream I was certainly scared," I said.

"Who do you think the surgeon is?" she asked, and I knew exactly what she meant. For she was also a surgeon. And there was no local anaesthetic to protect me from the pain of the knife she wielded. It was altogether natural to worry about a surgical procedure, no matter how minor; it was natural for me to be apprehensive about entering into a therapeutic relationship.

Released, I could finally reveal the source of my anger. And while I was casting about for the proper tones in which to couch my dangerous admission, I realized that there had always been two people sitting in the chair with me, answering Dr. Marks's questions. One was a spirited conversationalist who responded with irrepressible vivacity, honesty, and feeling. But she, unfortunately, could not speak aloud, and had instead to communicate first with someone in whose throat every sentiment became attenuated, and who spoke in a flat, dead, thin, dry voice: a censor's voice. This was the voice that explained to Dr. Marks, "It bothers me that you still look at the clock." Of course, the voice didn't sound angry, but rather assumed the detached, self-mocking tone of someone who expected praise for her honesty. But, for the first time, the views she expressed were unedited.

Concurrently, I understood that there were two therapists in the room with me — Dr. Marks, who never judged me, who never reacted in ways I could have predicted but never let me down; and the person I was always on the verge of expecting Dr. Marks to become, a woman who did nothing but judge me and react to me in horribly predictable ways.

Sometimes I would catch myself anticipating Dr. Marks's transformation. In the middle of a confession what I was saying would suddenly take on a much larger resonance, as if I had suddenly begun speaking through a megaphone, broadcasting backward in my life toward incidents long past. Both Dr. Marks and I would sit suspended as I tried to identify who I was really talking to. I felt at these moments like an archaeologist stumbling upon a mound that contained a wealth of relics — "We found it!" Now all we have to do is sift through the trove piece by piece, first removing the layer of soil that hides the treasure's real worth.

This sifting had to take place in the present tense, not in the past. Dr. Marks's job, I began to realize, was less to offer me structured interpretations — computer print-outs — than to let me talk to myself, or to whoever I imagined was sitting in her chair. Something would emerge from these conversations, something we would both witness, and make sense of together. She was there not to speculate on what made me tick but to listen; not to give answers, but to ask questions; the present mattered much more than the past; we weren't working in sequence but in tandem: in sum, everything I was so sure I understood about therapy had been perfectly wrong.

I hadn't even come to therapy for the reason I thought I had. These sessions were only tangentially for my son's sake. And there was one other truth I had stumbled onto, just before the holidays came and the Institute closed for two weeks, a truth that was melodramatic, even to me — I was thirty years old and I hadn't begun to know who I was.

VIII

THE WAITING ROOM of the Institute had never looked cozier; even the out-of-date, fraying magazines held promise. I had come for my first therapy session in three weeks directly from my post-op checkup with the surgeon who had performed hernia surgery on me. Admiring his stitchery, he announced proudly that everything was fine. When I complained of a numbness around the incision he assured me that it would soon disappear, though when I pressed him he confessed to not knowing its cause. "Had sex yet?" he asked. "You can, you know."

"But it still hurts."

"Well, what did you expect?" he said. "We cut you open."

His transformation stung me. I'd interviewed three surgeons before selecting him because he seemed so friendly, easygoing, reassuring, avuncular — many of the traits I'd hoped for in my therapist — but apparently only in the pre-op phase of his personality did he use gentle words like "discomfort" and "incision," lulling me into thinking that I'd walk away from the "procedure" needing only a Band-Aid. Now that his work was done he seemed almost scornful; his vocabulary had turned harsh, and he relished questioning me about my sexual activity. Was there a clinical reason for his inquiry, or was it simple prurience? Why did he dismiss my pain, my feelings? Why was he so inconsistent? "You can get dressed now," he said, lingering in the examination room. All I could think of was how much I longed, *longed*, for therapy.

Here was Dr. Marks, right on time. I followed her through the corridor to her office, barely restraining myself from launching into an account of the past three weeks as we were climbing the stairs.

I sat down, smiling, more than eager to begin.

"Do you mind if I tape our session?" Dr. Marks asked. She didn't look at me, but concentrated on untangling the cord of the small black cassette recorder that she had removed from her briefcase and placed on the wooden table between us.

"No," I said reflexively, as if my assent were a foregone conclusion, but in truth I simply didn't know what else to say. Why, I wondered, didn't she ask me how I was, how the operation had gone? I had been bursting with grist for the therapeutic mill. But now the presence of the tape recorder changed the complexion of the session and I was completely distracted. It wasn't stage fright or self-consciousness that stopped me from speaking. I was an incorrigible exhibitionist; in my parents' home movies I am always the child spinning around batting my eyelashes, smiling ingratiatingly, hogging the scene, wishing that the camera would keep its gaze on me forever. In fact, only a few weeks earlier I had wished that the sessions could be recorded, but on tapes I would take home and listen to, tapes that would help refresh my memory, become part of my personal archive, alongside my diaries. This tape, however, wasn't for me, but about me.

In a room in which even a piece of furniture could have significance, what enormous significance did a tape recorder have? Did Dr. Marks record all of her patients, or was I a particularly interesting case? Did having the tape release her from having to listen to me, allow her time to indulge in her own daydreams?

Where and when would she replay the tape? Was I to be part of a study, a monograph? Would she present me to her colleagues, at a seminar, at a supervision group, or was I to be listened to at home, during meals or before sleep, or through earphones on her bus trip to the office?

Why did she want to tape my session? It was a simple question. Yet I was as far from asking her that as I was from suddenly standing up and taking off all my clothes. Sure, she'd asked me if I minded, but that was nothing more than a rhetorical question. I had to answer yes. What other choice did I have? I certainly couldn't have begun to explain why I minded — I didn't know.

Questions spawned more questions, more suspicions. My cheeks felt hot, my mouth dry — the last time I'd felt this way was years before, ice-skating with my father, when I'd fallen and gotten the wind knocked out of me. I'd sat in the middle of the rink, unable to breathe or produce a single sound, while hundreds of people — including my own father! — skated around me as if I were invisible. Didn't he know I was dying?

Of course, eventually he skated over, explained what had happened, and got me back on my feet. But I'd never forgotten the shocking discovery that I could need him and he could *not know:* I may not have been able to talk, but still he should have heard me. Now too; Dr. Marks should have known that the tape recorder would send me into a tailspin. I felt angry, betrayed, hurt. How could she do this — surprise, abandon, confuse, me — especially now, so soon after my surgery?

The tape recorder sat between Dr. Marks and me, silently spinning. Gradually, my tongue loosened, and I began talking about something — certainly not the operation or my feelings concerning the tape recorder — convinced that my burgeoning agitation remained deep within me, unrecordable and undetectable, just as I had been convinced once years ago that my mother believed me when I explained that my brother was crying because he'd inexplicably hit himself in the head with a toy hammer.

A beep signaling that the tape had run out interrupted me; Dr. Marks grimaced and turned off the machine. Never one to overstay my welcome, I automatically swallowed the end of my sentence. We smiled conspiratorially at each other, acknowledging that the spoken content of our session was eminently forgettable. Still, I got up and left with a kind of bravado: considering the intensity of the emotional uproar I'd just experienced and all the millions of questions I had generated and suppressed, it was to my credit that I had managed to say anything at all.

Instead of sleeping in his crib, Ben sleeps on a shelf near our bed. He has a bad rash on his face; I must rub it with a special cream. Now Ben has changed into Jean, a close friend, who had a serious operation when I was pregnant with Ben; the rash is on her face. It won't wash off. I'm afraid of rubbing the cream into her face — what if I catch it?

"What do you think the dream is about?" Dr. Marks asked at our next session. I hated when she asked formal questions like that. Of course I didn't know what the dream was about — she knew this, and she also knew that I knew that she did.

"Tell me about your friend Jean. What kind of operation did she have?"

"An abdominal operation."

"Like yours," Dr. Marks said.

"Not really." Jean's was serious, life-threatening; it took hours and specialists and weeks of recuperation. Dr. Marks looked at me very seriously.

"And yours?"

Mine was nothing in comparison. Yet I still had a shudder of pain along the incision, which didn't bother me as much as the stubborn numbness surrounding it.

"Maybe you're still anaesthetized," Dr. Marks said.

Cute, I thought, looking up, expecting to find her smiling; instead, she looked almost stern.

"I guess I never told you about the operation," I admitted.

After an hour's wait in the crowded admissions office, David and I had been directed to take the red elevators to the third floor and from there to follow the green arrows to a ward containing four semiprivate rooms, all empty. Nurses and orderlies passed by only rarely; the corridor was silent and empty. I felt as if I had checked into a sanitorium.

David switched on the television, inspected the bathroom and closet, tugged on the window shade, and positioned the vinyl recliner near the lamp. These tiny adjustments rescued the nondescript, impersonal room from anonymity and made it ours. With similar touches he'd personalized hotel, pension, and bed-and-breakfast rooms across Europe during the summers we'd traveled; in fact, for a moment I felt a surge of romance, as if we were on a holiday.

But then a nurse appeared to take my temperature and blood pressure, an austere reminder that this was no idyll, that I was slated for surgery at ten the next morning. "You'll be more comfortable in your nighty, dear," she informed me, although it was three o'clock on a Sunday afternoon.

"You can go any time," I told David. I was worried about Ben, who was staying with my parents for the three days I'd be hospitalized, our longest separation. David nodded and dealt out our customary sections of the Sunday paper. At six he went to get take-out Chinese food, which he ate from the containers. At seven the surgeon appeared to describe the "procedure."

"She should be back in her room by noon," the doctor said to David, ignoring me, as if I were a child, or invisible. "Why don't you meet her here then?"

"I'll try to come earlier," David said, putting on his jacket. I assured him that I'd be just fine, that it didn't pay for him to come when I was still groggy. Anyway, I wanted him to stay with Ben.

"Ben will be fine," David said, leaning over, squeezing my hand. He was never comfortable with dramatic displays of affection, and tonight more than ever, I knew, he needed to obliterate the distance between this good-night and any other. As if he were simply going into the living room to watch television, he kissed me lightly and left.

Alone, I panicked. As an adult, I'd never been in a hospital except to have a baby, yet this hospital was horribly familiar to me: my cousin, a woman my age, had died here of cancer. Her room had been opposite a staff lounge, and I had spent most of my visits straining to hear the doctors' conversation just in case Lily's diagnosis came up over coffee and doughnuts. Once when I came to visit I brought her a box of stationery. I found her sitting up, addressing New Year's cards, which never got mailed.

Suddenly I felt possessed by her memory; I had to see the room where Lily had died. But as I was slipping on my robe, a nurse appeared and helped me back into bed. "No excursions now," she said. "We have to prep you for surgery." She produced a razor from a pocket in her uniform. I am being prepped for surgery, I repeated to myself; what has until now happened only to people I know is happening to me. I felt as if I were hovering a few inches above my body without being connected to it.

I remember thinking before I fell asleep that I should have told the surgeon that this was my second hernia operation; I'd had my first when I was only six months old. My mother tells the story of how I woke up from a nap feverish and inconsolable. She rushed me to the doctor, who rushed me to the hospital for emergency surgery. The story skips to the next morning when my parents came to visit me and found me, to everyone's amazement, standing up in the crib, completely recovered.

I knew what hospital cribs looked like — transparent plastic cages with no bumpers or decals on the headboard — and the linen was starchy white. Five days after Ben's birth he had to be rushed back to the hospital as an emergency admission for acute neonatal jaundice. His phototherapy lasted for three days and two nights. The pediatric wing had a lounge where parents could sleep. I slept at home. How could I have done that? How could I have left him? I cried, just before falling off to sleep. How could they — all of them, anyone, then or now — leave me?

I was sure that in the abandoned wing I'd be forgotten, but a nurse slipped into my room at dawn to wake me and give me a shot. Two men transferred me to a stretcher and wheeled me through crowded corridors to the operating room. The benefits of a local anaesthetic were these: I could hear the doctors talking, was aware of a drawing sensation in my abdomen, and could answer direct questions, such as, "Can you feel this?" Immediately after supplying my answer I drifted back into a deep reverie.

In the recovery room I heard hushed voices and saw a big clock, just like the one I had stared at during my labor. Then I was in motion again, being wheeled back to my room, and who should be there but David, who had come early, before visiting hours, even though the doctor and I had told him not to. He bent down to kiss me, and never in my life was I happier to see anyone.

But from that moment on my recovery went downhill. David stayed with me as I slept away the entire day. Friends called, flowers arrived, but everything came to me across an unbridgeable distance. My parents and in-laws, looking terribly uncomfortable, visited that night: they stood at the foot of my bed looking down at me, as if a chasm separated us, and wouldn't take off their coats. Ben, my parents assured me, was doing fine. I could see that he was exhausting them.

Dr. Marks had advised me to ask for pain medication if I

needed it, but when I asked the nurse for a pill that night she told me I'd heal faster if I foreswore it. Her tone and glance made me feel like a drug abuser.

The next morning my surgeon discharged me, telling me that I could resume sexual relations in a week. He wasn't the only upbeat one. "You're doing great," David said, his voice hurrying me along as I tried to maneuver my sore body into the car. Walking hurt. I sank into the passenger seat and tried not to think that I'd soon have to get out. On the drive to my parents' house I worried that Ben would be angry with me, that he would hang back, or cry. But no, he came running, delighted to see me. He pulled on my leg. I couldn't pick him up.

David helped me to a chair, put Ben on my lap, and suddenly announced that he was late for a meeting in the city which he swore he'd told me about. To go and leave me, today, already, like this? I had to fight back tears. Sure, my mother would be with me, but her patience was clearly flagging. "I'm just curious," she asked over lunch, "but when do you think you'll go back home?"

Listen, everyone, I felt like screaming, I just had an operation. It may not have been the most serious operation ever performed, but it was performed on *me*, and now I need just a few moments to convalesce: I ache, I'm tired, I'm scared.

I'd let the doctor convince me that the interval between surgery and recovery would be direct and brief. A victim of the doctor's misrepresentation and my own gullibility, I now found myself stuck on a train that was barreling too fast. I cried out for it to slow down, to make an unscheduled stop, but no one heard me; no one wanted to see that my recovery had derailed. I'd promised my family that I'd be back on my feet in no time, and they expected me to keep my word.

"Here too?" Dr. Marks asked. She'd been studying me very intently as I spoke. "Do you have to be back on your feet here as well?"

I blushed, felt my panic rising, just as I had when she asked if I minded having our sessions taped. When Dr. Marks posed questions like these I knew she was offering me something, something I wanted though I wasn't sure what it was or why I wanted it or what I'd do with it, or most important, why I had to refuse it. But to accept was out of the question, just as I couldn't accept a diamond from a suitor whose ardor scared me.

"No, not here," I said.

Dr. Marks smiled wanly; had I disappointed her? Wasn't this the assurance she wanted? I was very practiced at sniffing out the expected answer to just about any question: this sensitivity was something I prided myself on. Yet I felt as if I were sixteen again, trying to flirt with a boy I liked who had finally deigned to talk to me, only to have said something dumb.

But what could I have said? In a way this room was becoming a refuge for me; with its soft lighting and cushions, its warmth and conversation, it was the antithesis of that awful hospital room. I knew I could feel safe here, that I *should* feel safe here, but at the present moment I wasn't sure how I felt.

"I don't know what to say," I finally stammered. "I don't know how to answer your questions. I guess I don't think you mean them, or rather, that you ask them when you already know the answer."

She didn't say anything, and in the silence my mind raced on. Maybe it wasn't Dr. Marks who foreclosed on answers, but me. I never considered any question seriously. Instead, I was an expert at giving back the polite, expedient response. If Dr. Marks were to ask me if I was thirsty, I'd first consider the politics of the offer: Did she mean it? Why did she offer? What would it mean if I accepted? The question of whether or not I was thirsty wouldn't enter into my decision except as an afterthought.

"In fact," I said, "I'm not even sure I know when I am thirsty.

Or hungry." My family had led a scheduled life: we breakfasted, lunched, snacked, and supped at preordained hours. Spur-of-the-moment eating or drinking was regarded suspiciously. In my house no one thought it unusual to reply to the question, "Would you like a drink?" with, "No, I had something to drink an hour ago."

Dr. Marks laughed. "That sounds very routinized," she said. "And very rigid. No wonder you felt that you had to get better in a hurry. And no wonder you weren't sure how to talk about your pain with your family. You had to be more concerned with the effect of your pain on them."

Yes, yes, yes. That was exactly right. I found myself shivering as I often did at moments when I knew that I had made myself understood. Dr. Marks heard me; she put my pain into words and presented them to me so that I could see outside myself.

"You were right," I said, not looking at her — somehow, I'd lost track of how we'd circled back to the operation, to my abridged convalescence — "the operation was horrible. It still is. I feel raw, exposed all over, just as you said."

Meeting Dr. Marks's eyes, I saw for the first time what she was offering me. This was a room, she seemed to be saying, where I could pay attention to my own pain without worrying about its impact on anyone else. I could get off my feet, kick off my shoes, curl up in a fetal position on her couch, and whimper. I would have done it, too, except I seemed powerless to move, as if my spinal cord were severed and my body were no longer receiving messages from my brain.

Just then the tape recorder clicked off. Neither of us moved. "I don't feel like leaving tonight," I said finally, in a dull voice, bitterly regretting the opportunity I had just squandered. Dr. Marks shifted her weight in her chair and smiled her our-session-is-over smile, ejecting the cassette from the machine and placing it in her briefcase.

"See you next time," she said.

IX

FOR MONTHS I'd been waiting for the perfect moment to tell my parents that I'd begun therapy — a quiet moment when I could trust that I'd stay calm in the face of their nearly imperceptible reaction. The momentary flicker of tension washing across their faces I could tolerate; their denial of this tension was what always proved incendiary to me.

Yet after all my careful planning I couldn't have picked a more improbable time — in the midst of Ben's first birthday party. A nervous host under the best of circumstances, I felt particularly besieged that day. Our tiny apartment was overrun by the seven members of our immediate families who had come for lunch; and Ben, dispensing with his regular nap, was maddeningly underfoot all morning, a voracious bundle of appetite. Finally my parents volunteered to take him outside for a stroll. The first course wasn't even on the table when I heard Ben's cries rising up the elevator shaft.

"He only wants to walk," my mother said. Both she and my father seemed cross and tired. "It's impossible to take him out anymore." Ben had wriggled out of his jacket and held one shoe in his hand; he clung to me as I untangled his seat belt. Always a physically precocious child, standing at five months, crawling at six, Ben had taken his first steps days after he turned nine months old. Since that moment he'd had nothing but disdain for his stroller, tolerating it for only ten minutes at a time, demanding the rights of a miniature person. Unleashed on the street, he would dart athwart the pavement with no sense of direction or purpose, in and out of people's paths, a tiny, menacing commando, bent on creating chaos.

You can't be proud of him for learning to walk and angry at him for wanting to, I silently said to my parents, as I served lunch with Ben on my hip.

Eventually Ben fell asleep; in fact, he overslept, giving both sets of grandparents and his great-grandmother ample opportunity to stand over his crib, punctuating their adoration with anxious questions: "Is he all right?" "Do you think he's warm enough?" "Does he usually sleep this long?"

These questions were irksome to me, I knew, because I entertained them myself. No one scrutinized Ben more than I did; no one was more sensitive to the most minute fluctuations in his behavior. Why did I find such concern — and pride — coming from anyone other than myself so unwholesome?

Or was it simply that my parents, with whom I'd been getting along harmoniously for the past six years, could suddenly do nothing right? This too puzzled me, for I'd never appreciated or loved them more than now that I had a child of my own to protect, to love and fret over, now that I was experiencing from the inside all that they had sacrificed and given me. They felt about me the way I felt about Ben. This simple analogy enabled me to understand their fearfulness, their protectiveness, their ambivalent attitude toward my ever-increasing independence. Yet I also couldn't completely stifle the feeling that any moment, in response to what they would deem a perfectly innocuous question, I'd break out in a full-blown case of age-inappropriate adolescence right before all our eyes.

Maybe this was because in the year since my son's birth I'd seen more of my parents than I had since I'd left their house for college thirteen years ago. We had fallen into a pattern of regular visits. Every Saturday at two o'clock they'd appear at my door:

"Did we wake the baby?" they'd always ask instead of saying hello, with exaggerated concern, as if waking him was a crime from which there'd be no absolution.

They'd bring a jumbo box of disposable diapers, an outfit for Ben or a toy my father had handcrafted in his basement carpentry shop, and a treat from the bakery or some homemade soup for David and me. Silent, they bustled around the tiny apartment putting everything away, shrugging off my thanks as if their generosity were a reflex rather than voluntary, taking a drink, washing their hands, and finally tiptoeing in to see Ben, who had slept through their arrival, after all.

"Will you come to the park with us?" my mother asked every week, her question invariably giving me pause. For as grateful as I felt for their visits, and as much as I enjoyed walking with them and having adult company in the playground, what I really wanted was to stay home, blissfully alone.

"We'll be back in an hour or two," my father assured me, taking his position behind the stroller.

Don't hurry, I said, not aloud of course, thinking of the heroine's cinematic gesture as she not only closes the door but throws her back up against it as well.

Before I could read the newspaper, wash the dishes, go through the week's mail, they'd all be back — my parents and Ben from their expedition, David from the library where he'd been working on his thesis. Then it would be time to take our places for the event we coproduced each week: David's and my night out. David would lose himself in the restaurant guides and yellow pages, selecting our cuisine and making the reservation; my parents would eat an early dinner in the kitchen; and I'd bathe Ben, preoccupied by thoughts of what dress to wear, which perfume to dab, which earrings to put on, obsessively considering each detail as if I were preening for my first date.

For all his prowess as a mind reader, Ben always seemed particularly dense on Saturday nights, unable or unwilling to sense my impatience to get him out of the bath and into his pajamas. He'd stand at attention in the corner of his crib, watching me nervously, fully aware that my primping would all too soon culminate in a moment he loathed: my saying good-bye.

In the living room, David habitually scribbled phone numbers on a napkin — the restaurant, our neighbors, the police precinct, the pediatrician, poison control. My mother would shrug and ask, "What could happen?"

As I buttoned my coat Ben inevitably began to cry. I'd hesitate, David's cue to hustle me out the door. "A crisp good-bye," he advised. No one in my family knew what that meant. My father, looking stricken, held Ben at the threshold, asking me with his eyes how I could even think of leaving, how I could bear upsetting my little boy so terribly, my precious little son who loves me so.

David would lock the door behind us. I'd ask if we couldn't wait until we heard Ben stop wailing; in response he'd brusquely marshal me into the elevator. I knew that he resented having to drag me out of the house every week. "He'll be fine," David would say, as we settled into a taxi. "He always is."

In the past months we had spent a small fortune on restaurants and taxis, probably more than we had spent during the five years of the no-frills life we had led until Ben's birth. Saturday nights out used to mean dinner at a tiny, overcrowded, noisy Chinese restaurant, which we had reached by taking subways and walking. Now the prospect of such an evening depressed me. I wanted to take taxi cabs to and from quiet, tasteful restaurants whose ambience I once shunned. I wanted to be pampered: easy transportation, expensive food, new clothes and jewelry, facials, manicures, pedicures, beauty treatments I scarcely knew about. And if these desires weren't strange enough, I felt passionately entitled to luxury. After all, I'd been assiduously thrifty for years and years; surely this counted for some kind of credit.

But in reality, money had never been tighter. All week I worried about the bills we were incurring, only to watch each Saturday night as David blithely signed away yet another precious and unjustifiably large portion of our meager weekly salary.

Still, the few hours we spent together on Saturday nights was the highlight of the week, the best time until next week. Sometimes I wished we could window-shop and walk all night and wake up in a hotel room, victims of an overpowering amnesia.

When we'd arrive back at our apartment well before midnight, my mother would be reading, my father napping, our son fast asleep in his crib. "He cried a bit after you left," my father would report, "but eventually we got him to quiet down." They packed their books and magazines, slipped on their shoes, and walked into their grandson's bedroom one at a time to get one last dose of angelic sweetness. Sometimes I wondered if they didn't love him best when he was clean and asleep.

After they'd leave I'd feel ridiculously like Cinderella. The jewelry I couldn't wear tending to a baby — rings, long chains — went back in the jewelry box. I washed my mascara off with baby oil. The sweatshirt and jeans I always wore were still on the chair where I had thrown them hours before.

David would be reading the paper in bed. In five and a half hours Ben would be up clamoring for milk, attention, games. My eyes would close as I tried to do the crossword puzzle; the sports section David was reading would fall from his hands.

"I've had it," he'd say, taking off his glasses. I too was exhausted. But I didn't want the night to end.

"Let's hear the news," I'd suggest, though I was hopelessly out of date on current events and didn't really care. All I needed was to be awake another few moments, aware that I was tending to no one.

But David would yawn and turn out the light. What a swell time we had, we'd tell each other. A moment later he'd be asleep, and I'd be up, sometimes for what felt like hours.

Sleep always eluded me Saturday nights. Often I thought about those rare weekends when my parents would leave me at my grandparents' overnight. These visits always began well: I relished the cookies my grandmother baked for me, the way she washed me with a stiff washcloth, the novelty of sleeping in a new bed with those crisp, icy sheets, the sound of my grandparents having breakfast together at six in the morning. But after my grandfather and I had returned from our Sunday morning walk to the candy store, where he had bought me some comic books, and he had finished reading the funny papers to me, I'd start to worry out loud. Shouldn't my parents have been here by now? What if they never came back?

They always did, of course, and each time my grandmother told them what a nervous state I'd worked us all into. My parents were angry, but didn't say so; instead, they acted disappointed. Eventually the overnights stopped.

Did my parents resent the fact that the same child who made it so hard for them to leave could now leave her own child so easily? Did they know that I never left easily, that my only advantage was in having David, who believed in saying good-bye and shutting the door? His ear couldn't discern the inaudible plea wafting across the generations in my family, the message that came to me from my parents, who'd heard it from theirs, the message I was trying so desperately to keep from Ben: "Never leave," they chorused, "please never leave."

I was brewing coffee and sticking candles in the birthday cake when David found me ruminating in the kitchen. "Come on," he said, "we're going out."

"We can't go out now," I reminded him as if he were slow-witted, "Ben will be up any minute. This is his birthday party."

"But it's not his only party," David reminded me. In a week, we'd celebrate Ben's birthday again, with over thirty friends and relatives gathered at my mother's house. "Let's just pick up some Chinese food for dinner tonight. Come on, it's a shame to have so many babysitters in one room and not take advantage of them."

It sounded heretical to me. But I was feeling nervous, and that made me reckless. We appeared in the living room, amid our family, in our coats. "We'll be back soon," we promised, and out we went.

A date — in the middle of the afternoon! We walked down the block with our arms around each other, heading, I assumed, for the neighborhood restaurant. But after crossing Broadway, David hailed a cab. "Chinatown," he said, before I could protest.

"Don't worry," David said.

"How do you know I'm worrying?"

"Your mouth tightens up."

"We'll be gone at least an hour, this cab ride alone will cost — "

"Are you having a good time? What would you rather do with the money we are so wantonly squandering now?" David was very levelheaded about finances. He also knew that I knew that none of my visions of penury had ever materialized.

"Save it," I said instantly.

"For what?" he asked, unaware that this was a ridiculous question. Money should be saved; that was one of the axioms of my upbringing.

The city streets were congested; Chinatown itself was like a parking lot. Instead of ordering from one restaurant David insisted that we go to four, culling our favorite dishes from each, a bountiful Chinese smorgasbord. The sky was dusky by the time we found a cab to take us back uptown.

"Don't worry," David said. "Sometimes you just have to tune out other people's expectations. That's what I've been talking about in therapy."

David was uncharacteristically closemouthed about his therapy; he didn't share my enthusiasm for comparing notes. Only once in a great while, usually at the damnedest moments — in a cab speeding uptown with Chinese food leaking onto our laps, for example — would the thoughts he'd been percolating boil over into a conversation for which I was never prepared.

"I've been talking about that too," I said, seizing the opportunity. "But about three weeks ago Dr. Marks started taping my sessions, and for some reason that really makes me clam up."

"Yeah, mine are being taped, too." We were stuck in traffic at Times Square. "Actually, I'm going to start going twice a week," David said.

Twice a week? His news hit me with the force of a blow. In my struggle to regain internal equilibrium I couldn't begin to understand exactly what about his announcement had upset me; I only realized that these past weeks — since my operation — I'd been feeling as if I were walking through life with my forearms folded over my chest in an attempt to ward off a barrage of changes that were relentlessly being thrown at me. A tape recorder, a husband who made a personal decision without consulting me, a birthday party — these were all conspiring to undo me.

I was on the verge of telling David how fragile, how brittle I felt these days, but just then the taxi swerved left toward the highway, throwing both of us violently off balance. By the time we had rearranged ourselves and checked the shopping bags of food, I could read in David's eyes that our conversation about therapy was over.

Our families greeted us with a stony silence. Ben had woken up from his original nap and was now back to sleep, "Happy Birthday" had been sung, the cake cut and eaten, presents opened, photographs snapped, and we, the parents, had missed it all.

"I don't understand you," my father said, when he and my

mother found me in the kitchen rinsing plates. From his averted eyes and his heavy voice I knew he was deeply disappointed.

In his hands was the piece of paper with which he'd meticulously wrapped Ben's present, creasing the corners and matching the pattern as if he were hanging wallpaper. Somehow he'd salvaged it from Ben's greedy grasp, hoping to teach his grandson that in our family we don't hatchet open presents; instead, we gingerly unpeel them, as if they are delicate fruits.

"Look, I'm in therapy," I said, snatching the wrapping paper out of his hand, the paper I was supposed to save and recycle; I crumbled it up and threw it away, an action that astonished all three of us. I looked at him with baleful sixteen-year-old eyes; his, in answer, were plaintive: Why are you making us read through this script a second time? Wasn't the original performance of your adolescence more than enough?

X

"DAVID'S GOING to therapy twice a week," I announced to Dr. Marks before she had gotten comfortable in her chair. I felt curiously, recklessly free plunging into the session, abandoning the graceful entrance I was accustomed to staging. My words sounded so impolite, so assertive.

"Oh?" Dr. Marks said.

I'd come to anticipate the neutrality of her interjections, her blankness a kind of sieve through which only my literal words passed, the tone in which I'd delivered them and the lumpen mess of feelings which I'd meant to imply remaining behind for further inspection. "How does that make you feel?" she asked after a suitable pause, forcing me to examine my motives, to make infuriatingly explicit what in any other conversation with any other person could remain conveniently tacit.

There I sat, stewing in emotion, and Dr. Marks wanted me to enumerate my feelings one by one, as if I were compiling a shopping list. The exercise seemed pointless: anger melded with envy, and envy with fear, as if they were seasonings in the hands of a skillful chef. As much as I admired those culinary detectives who could discern single ingredients amid a savory welter of flavors, my own taste buds were too underdeveloped to pinpoint the pinch of marjoram or the dash of sherry, and I had similar trouble isolating my emotions. What I was feeling was — what? With a shock I realized that I didn't know.

As the mother of a toddler I spent twelve hours a day following my son around: he'd point; I'd name. In this way objects acquired a reality they didn't have for him the moment before I named them. Knowing their names gave him power, and he was hungry for it. Yet here I sat, powerless, bereft, unable to supply names for the very feelings holding me captive, knowing as little about them as my son would know about the world if I had taken him to the park and merely said, "Things." Without names my feelings weren't mine to claim; weren't, in some crucial way, *real*.

Hadn't anyone ever taken me on a walk through my emotions? Was this what Dr. Marks was trying to do? Her annoying question wasn't intended to have me report what I already knew; she was asking me to discover what I didn't know. As a writing teacher I'd always assured my students that writing is less an exercise in transcribing into words what we've already worked out in our heads than a process by which we discover what we want to say. And we learn what we mean by writing it down. Or saying it aloud. "How does that make you feel?"

In the stumbling way that toddlers walk, I began to explain. That David had made such an enormous decision without consulting me made me feel angry and betrayed. An extra session for him would strain not only our budget but our schedule, and the burden of finding the extra money and time would fall on me. And that made me feel resentful.

That I didn't know who had suggested the extra session made me curious and anxious. How had it even come up? If his therapist suggested it I felt envious, but also nervous; what if she thought he needed the extra help? Worse, what if David had suggested it? What if his problems were more deep-seated than I knew; what if he were more troubled than I realized? Part of me envied David his more serious problems. But wait — what if he actually found the help he needed? Would he still love me? Cured of his neuroses, would he still need me?

Great. Now my feelings had names — anger, anxiety, envy, fear — and they were such a disgusting, sordid catalogue that I felt sick acknowledging them. What could Dr. Marks possibly think of me?

"How do you feel about coming twice a week?" Dr. Marks asked.

"I can't," I instantly replied, frantically casting about for a reason to cite. "We can't afford it."

"Money is the problem?" Dr. Marks asked.

The Institute determined payment on a sliding scale. Even though we qualified for the lowest rung, the monthly bills were liquidating our savings; additional sessions would accelerate the process.

"It's not just the money," I said, as it grew suddenly sickeningly clear that it was, though perhaps not in the way I originally intended. I felt like a hapless sleuth who thought she'd discovered the shortest way out of the haunted house only to have stepped on a loose plank and landed in the dark, dank cellar. How could I claim hardship for myself when I knew that David hadn't for a moment stopped to think that we couldn't afford his extra session? To complain about having to pay for therapy seemed very bad form; as it was, we paid less than anyone we knew. *What's wrong with you?* a voice snarled. *Do you expect to get therapy for free?*

Cowering, I looked up, expecting to see in Dr. Marks's eyes the contempt I had heard in her voice. But she hadn't spoken. The attack on me came from within; the excoriating tone was my own. Not until Dr. Marks asked, in her modulated way, "What is it then?" did I realize how I always expected her to assault me verbally, the way I had assaulted myself.

"I'm not sure," I said, but suddenly, almost forcibly, my concentration shifted. Years ago, when I was still a size 6X, my grandmother had taken me shopping for a party dress. The one I picked out was pink, replete with crinolines and lace trim and a satin bow around the waist. I remembered admiring myself in front of the three-way mirror, twirling around to see the skirts billow, and knowing that no matter what — no matter how cheaply the dress was made or how overpriced it was — my grandmother would buy it for me.

Dr. Marks smiled.

On the other hand, I ploughed on, I remembered many other scenes in department stores, shopping for school wardrobes, with my parents. Free to make my own selections, I innocently but invariably was drawn to the most expensive sweater or skirt or pair of shoes, forcing my parents to make an anguished decision. Was it worth getting? Would I wear it enough to justify the expense? Was there another item like it at a more reasonable price?

"Yet I never heard the words 'We can't afford it,' " I said.

"You were supposed to intuitively know the limits of your parents' budget," Dr. Marks commented.

Yes, that was it exactly; Dr. Marks's ability to encapsulate what I was trying to say made me shiver, her insights as sharp and clear as ice. Suddenly, instead of being the villain of my anecdote I was its innocent victim: how could I have known about money when it was never discussed with me? My problem wasn't simply that I had had extravagant tastes, but that these tastes forced my parents to impose limits, something they had difficulty doing. If I had been more reasonable about the clothes I selected, they wouldn't have had to deny me, and then we could have all pretended that we could have whatever we wanted.

Yet confounding the already knotty scenario was the fact that my parents usually ended up granting my wish: the sweater or pair of shoes I had mulishly coveted were almost always ultimately mine.

"Maybe money wasn't the whole issue," Dr. Marks said. I nodded, barely acknowledging her; that had just dawned on me too. Her voice seemed to come not from across the room but from inside me, her commentary woven into my own internal monologue, which was rapidly unfolding. I didn't know where I was headed, could barely keep up with myself, yet she was keeping pace with me, noticing the tiny details in the shadows, which I would have missed if I'd been alone, details that assumed massive significance the moment she pointed them out.

"I'm thinking about that party dress your grandmother bought for you," she continued. Yes: the dress I spontaneously wanted and instantly received. These were the issues my parents had trouble with — not money, for they were very generous people and never stinted on my brother or me, but spontaneity, desire. Their conferences in department store aisles were not convened to discuss budgetary problems but to slow me down, to stem the whirlwind of unbridled appetite that I must have embodied.

"She didn't hesitate," I said, thinking of my grandmother, my father's mother, the one I was supposed to take after. We were both tall and wiry; she'd had red hair as a girl, and so had I. Yet often she embarrassed me. On many occasions throughout my childhood she spread her more than ample lap wide enough to accommodate her six grandchildren at once and said, quite seriously, "I love you all but the first one is special." She meant me, her oldest grandchild.

"Listen to how you're speaking now," Dr. Marks said. She was leaning forward, close enough to touch me. My voice had dropped off. "You sound as if you're betraying a secret."

My grandmother hadn't known the meaning of secret. She would announce her preference at the drop of a hat.

"So what is the secret?" Dr. Marks asked.

Did she really not know? "I feel like I was everybody's favorite," I said, so softly that even I could barely hear myself.

Suddenly I was in my parents' house; I was sixteen. It was a spring night. My father and I had been fighting for days about whether or not I had permission to go to Woodstock. We met by chance in the foyer leading to all three bedrooms, both in our pajamas. I announced that I was going with all my friends, that he couldn't do anything to stop me. He said, "You're forcing me to abdicate my responsibility." He was nearly in tears.

Forcing him. I could do that. I must have my way. And I did.

"So you have a lot of power in your family," Dr. Marks said.

How did we get here so quickly? This was the secret that was supposed to take years of therapy to unlock. What was there left to talk about now?

"How does that make you feel?" Dr. Marks asked.

"Awful," I cried, "like a monster." The shrewish voice I'd heard a few minutes before had always been relentless on the subject of my rapacity. "Like I want too much, like I am too much."

"Do you worry that you're too much for me?" Dr. Marks asked. Without fully understanding what she meant, I knew that the answer was no.

That night, I stood for a few minutes outside the Institute on the corner across from Central Park feeling clean and wonderfully blank, as if I hadn't been sitting in one place for the past forty-five minutes but had instead just completed a ten-mile run. I hailed a cab, a rare indulgence when I was alone, and as I settled back in the seat, the decrepit metered taxi became a chauffeured limousine and I felt up to my neck in luxury. For the few minutes that it took the cab to travel up and across town I barely moved, as if the session — all its words and segues and relevations — were an almost palpable yet frangible creation entrusted to me for safekeeping.

But no sooner had I unlocked the door to my apartment than the buzz of family life assaulted me and my parcel, so carefully preserved inside me, not so much shattered as evaporated. I made a great show of sitting down at my desk with my coat on and reaching for my journal to record what had just transpired, but as soon as my pen was in my hand I knew that what I was about to write would have as little sense as a dream: from the therapy session I'd just left I could possibly retrieve an image or line of dialogue, but the evanescent context in which they belonged was beyond transcription or my powers of evocation.

"I can't see it," I said. I was having coffee with Martha, from my mothers' group, in a small pastry shop near my house, which was popular with college students. In twenty minutes we had to pick up our children at day care. "I mean, I wish I had the luxury of going twice a week, but I don't."

"You can make time, can't you?" Martha said. Inspired, she said, by me and our discussion in group a few months ago, she was now in therapy three mornings a week.

I stirred my café au lait. "It's not only the time," I admitted. "There's also the money."

She didn't reply. Another excuse, I knew she was thinking. But it was different for her. She loved her therapist. Even *I* loved her therapist: he was in his sixties, and he sounded wise and comforting, along the lines of my college therapist but without the hint of lechery. Martha confessed that she had a knack for finding such men. When she'd had a breakdown during college and spent two weeks in the hospital, the therapist who'd treated her literally saved her life, she insisted. Upon her release, he'd given her his home phone number and told her to call whenever she needed to. One night during a blizzard she'd found herself in the grip of an intense anxiety attack and called him and he'd said he'd meet her in his office at midnight. When she arrived twenty minutes late, nearly frozen — the busses had stopped running — he was waiting for her with a cup of cocoa. They had a wonderful session.

"I can't begin to imagine that," I said sadly. I had a hard enough time asking for help with physical emergencies, much less psychic ones: once during college I'd woken up unable to move out of my bed — an old back injury acting up — and rather than call my friend down the hall I waited, in pain, for two hours until she knocked on my door wondering why in the world I hadn't been at breakfast. To have a need as great as the one Martha described for something as intangible as emotional succor, and to be able to act on it, seemed quite beyond me.

"You're healthier than I am, that's all," Martha said. "Not that it's a contest. Your biggest problem is that you won't accept help even when it's being shoved in your face. And it has nothing to do with time or money, does it?"

Without looking up, I shook my head. Why couldn't Martha be my therapist, I wondered. I could talk freely to her. And for some reason she was expert at reading me.

I found myself staring at our waitress taking a break at a table in the back, frantically puffing on her cigarette and gulping her coffee. Time was running out; soon we'd have to leave, pick up our children, return to our separate homes, wait a whole week to talk again.

"But I don't know if I *need* to go more than once a week," I said, unable to keep the whine out of my voice. "If Dr. Marks told me that she thought I needed to come more often, I would. But she only brought it up because I did, and I brought it up because of David."

Martha was silent. To think about David's going to therapy twice a week and then about whether I wanted to go twice a week caused a bodily reaction with which I was all too familiar, having just stopped breast-feeding a few months before: I itched all over, felt parched and panic-riddled. The hormone that soothed most nursing mothers had agitated me, made me desperate to slip out of my body or else run the risk of being sucked dry. All I could think of were the ways in which two therapy sessions a week would drain me: another demand, one more activity to make time for, to finance, to squeeze in, to negotiate for. As if hundreds of babies were crawling on me, crying for me, clamoring for my milk, I found the prospect simply too exhausting and distasteful to think about.

"And what about what you would get out of it?" Martha asked quietly. "What about the ways therapy supports you, enriches you, fills you up, helps you?"

That's fine for you to say, I thought to myself — you like your therapist and he likes you. Yet I remembered how I had felt stepping out into the night air after my last therapy session, during the cab ride home, how peaceful I'd felt and how blessedly silent the world had seemed, every nagging voice inside me dramatically stilled. I had felt, I realized, as if I had taken a tiny sip of a cool, delicious beverage, both a stimulant and a relaxant. And I had to admit that the draft was intoxicating.

"Time to run," Martha said, signaling for the waitress. Casually I reached for the check, but Martha snatched it away. "Save your pennies," she said.

"I wish you would just tell me that you think it would be helpful for my therapy if I came twice a week," I told Dr. Marks at our next visit. "I'm great at doing my assignments."

Dr. Marks smiled an I'm-not-your-teacher-and-this-isn't-school smile. If only it were! I'd always been an excellent student; teachers doted on me. Not only did I fulfill expectations, but I could anticipate them, respond to them in advance, without being asked. Mrs. Brown, my second grade teacher, once asked me to clean the sink in the back of the room. Inspecting my work, she told me I'd done an impeccable job. "Does anyone know what 'impeccable' means?" she asked the class. No one did. I nearly swooned to realize that she needed a new word to express how well I had performed.

A performance indeed; in retrospect, it seemed that I excelled less at mastering any particular subject matter than at figuring out how to please the teacher. My entire distinguished academic career suddenly seemed to boil down to this bargain: tell me what I have to do to earn an A, and I'll do it.

How did I earn my A here? That Dr. Marks thought I should come twice a week seemed clear, though she hadn't admitted it aloud. But maybe she'd be prouder of me if I asserted my reluctance, if I resisted her.

"Look," I said finally, "I just don't think that I'm that troubled. I mean, I have a family and a job and friends. It's not like my life is falling apart. What will I talk about for ninety minutes a week?"

I couldn't admit to Dr. Marks, as I had to Martha over coffee, that I was afraid of being overwhelmed by therapy, afraid of drowning, afraid that the life I had just alluded to would come apart at the seams if I were to be in this office a minute longer than I was now. At the same time, I felt myself yearning for her to override me, to interrupt me, to assure me that she knew what was good for me — she could have even used the tone parents always use — and I would have obeyed.

"Are you afraid that we won't have enough to talk about?" Dr. Marks asked, unruffled. Yes, no, I don't know. I crossed my feet and sat up and slouched back down, sighed, and realized that I was having a muted version of a temper tantrum, just like the lovely two-year-old girl living in my building, who in the throes of her rage screamed a savage, NO! to every question her patient parents put to her — "Do you want to go to the park? Do you want a drink?" — the moment it was asked, before she had even considered the answer, even those to which she so obviously wanted to say yes.

"Do you think you have to have only one feeling?" Dr. Marks asked. Of course I didn't; I was a student of English literature, I knew all about ambivalence. "But you think you are exempt from it? Or do you think that you're not entitled to want what you want?"

"But what I want is a fantasy," I said despairingly. There, I'd said it, the single word that unclamped my imagination. In a rush it was clear to me what I wanted: to come five days a week, to sleep on her couch, to talk nonstop, *for free*, to have her cancel all her other clients, to take me out for lunch, for dinner, to adopt me, to show me her apartment, to welcome me into her life.

"Just because they're fantasies doesn't mean you can't harbor them," Dr. Marks said. "Just because you can't have your needs fulfilled doesn't mean you don't have them."

No one had ever said this to me. I had only the vaguest sense of what she meant; I couldn't yet allow myself to completely understand her. If I did, I might find myself in a haven I didn't know existed and wouldn't want to leave.

XI

A YEAR AGO I never would have approached her. I would have paused, peered through the store window to ascertain her identity, and kept walking. But for some reason, this April afternoon, I stopped and opened the door of the stationery store because my favorite college professor, Dr. Diana Holmes, was standing in one of the aisles examining black-and-white composition notebooks.

I introduced myself. Removing her glasses and collapsing them with one hand, she scratched her head with an eyepiece as she studied me, a very familiar gesture. "Yes, of course," she said. I knew she was picturing exactly where I had sat during her seminar. "How very nice to see you." Then she asked if it had been two or three years since I had graduated.

It had been ten.

"You don't look it," she said, several times. She did. Her face was heavily lined and her hair quite gray. Twelve years had passed since she had taught me Shakespeare.

I'd always emulated my English teachers. Mrs. Thompson, who, I later realized, must have been in her early fifties, launched her eighth grade class into a unit on death. I can recall her shade of lipstick just as clearly as I can hear her intoning the darker poems of Dickinson, Donne, and Shakespeare. I remember how the young, raven-haired woman who taught me Greek literature filed her long, squared-off fingernails. And just re-

cently, a picture of a pair of Belgian loafers in a clothing catalogue summoned up the willowy, sandy-haired woman who recited lines from the Bible in a resonant yet quivering voice.
These women seemed unshackled from their domestic lives,
and I memorized their wardrobes and personal grooming habits
along with their words. Their devotion to their careers mesmer-
ized me; the comfort, the sheer pleasure they derived from literature, inspired me.

Dr. Holmes interrupted my ruminations by asking what I was
up to these days. I told her that I was teaching freshman composition and writing as an adjunct instructor at two local colleges.

"You can teach without your doctorate?" The surprise in her
voice nonplussed me, for she had been the one who assured me
that I could. "Follow your heart," she had earnestly advised me
during my senior year when I came to her in a fit of indecision.
Though I'd always planned to pursue graduate study in English
literature, an unfortunate incident in my senior English seminar
had soured me on the prospect. What I wanted to do instead
was attend a creative writing program to see if my writing skills
could be honed. Yet I knew that ultimately I wanted to teach, to
one day have a desk and an office, a specialty and expertise like
hers, and that a doctorate, not a master's, was my only sure
ticket.

She had drawn her chair close to mine. "You'll get where you
want by doing what you want to do, not what you think you
should do," she said, perhaps sensing that graduate school in
my frame of mind would have proved disastrous. She promised
I'd find a way to accomplish everything I wanted. And so I went
off to study writing, with her blessing.

"Are you still writing?" she asked.

I hesitated — what did she mean? I hadn't written the novel
that I dreamt of in her office. Some of my articles and essays had
been appearing in women's magazines. She, on the other hand,

was a first-rate scholar and prolific writer; her articles on Shake-speare were very highly regarded. When I had been in her class she was in the midst of writing a book about *Othello*. Yes, I finally admitted, I'd been writing some short stories, a few of which had been published.

"I always wanted to write fiction." She spoke softly, her voice flat and breathy, almost a monotone. That was how she had recited Shakespeare, foreswearing any drama, each word plain and distinct, with cushions of air on each side so that the sound could sink in, almost as haltingly as a foreigner would read. Hers was an austere, cerebral Shakespeare, one that had nothing to do with props and stage business but only with language, and I've never gotten it out of my ears: to me, it's how the plays should sound. In fact, there are times when a performance or a recording of a Shakespeare play irritates me — the actors sound so overly dramatic.

"Are you married?" she asked. I told her about David and Ben.

"I wanted children, a slew of children, actually, ten or twelve. But I never had any."

For a few moments I thought she wouldn't speak again. I didn't know in which direction to steer the conversation; she had always been in charge of that. During the year that I was her student I met with her almost weekly, ostensibly to review the brief papers she assigned, but mostly just to talk. I didn't get along with most of my other English professors. Not only did they seem inordinately cliquish and stuck-up, but none of them admired my work: In the critical writing course required of all majors I received a B−, which, my professor tartly informed me, was the equivalent of a D. My eminent American literature professor and I didn't see eye to eye about Melville. Yet it wasn't until my senior year that my academic career plummeted to its nadir — the most flamboyant member of the English faculty returned the paper I had written for his seminar with a crisp note in lieu of a grade, reminding me that the purchase of term papers violated the college's code of ethics and subjected me to academic sanctions.

I was mortified. The classmates, friends, and boyfriend to whom I showed the paper were outraged. I took my case to the woman who co-taught the class, a very ambitious and prominent scholar, but she refused to dissent from her senior colleague's assessment. I shouldn't have been surprised; in class she would let him ramble on until he sat back exhausted from his ad-lib erudition and declared, "Enough," expansively leaving her the last fifteen minutes of a two-hour seminar in which to cram her twenty pages of prepared lecture notes.

In a white fury I visited the professor during his office hours, and presented him with my rough copy. Barely glancing at the yellow legal sheets and dismissing my explanation, he took the paper, inked a hasty C+ at the top of the page, and extended it across his desk without looking at me. When I asked for an apology he told me that I shouldn't look a gift horse in the mouth.

From there I fled to Dr. Holmes's office, my only on-campus sanctuary. She sat in her lopsided swivel chair in front of a desk strewn with papers. When she saw that I'd been crying she fixed me a cup of tea on a hot plate she kept on the windowsill. Her mug had lipstick stains all around it, as did her cigarettes. She used kitchen matches to light up and tossed them, without looking, into a white ceramic ashtray on a nearby bookcase. Her aim, as she read through my paper, was perfect.

Exhaling smoke through her nose like a steam engine, she told me she found the paper to be excellent. She tried to explain why a man like my professor couldn't back down. I told her I was tempted to go public, give my story to the college newspaper. She suggested that I might want to consult with the dean of studies (I did both, to no avail or personal satisfaction). I knew she felt terrible on my behalf.

Of course what I didn't tell her, during our cozy chat, was the extent to which I was consumed with fantasies of retribution. I swore I'd spit at him the next time I saw him, or trip him, or denounce him at the next faculty meeting. In my mind I drafted letters reminding him that his execrable act would never be forgotten or forgiven, but would remain emblazoned in my mind.

At the time, I didn't have to stop and consider why this incident so inflamed me; that seemed self-evident. But now, ten years later, I still hated him, and the wound he had inflicted still smarted. Why? I asked myself in a familiar voice — Dr. Marks's voice — and realized with a start that this entire encounter would soon be dissected in her office, where, I hoped, I'd finally be able to put it behind me. To Dr. Marks alone I could admit what I'd never been able to admit before — that although I had written the paper myself, and certainly hadn't plagiarized, I could have footnoted both more generously and more accurately. My disgrace wasn't entirely undeserved. However offensive the professor had been, his only real crime was in calling me aloud what I had previously called myself in private — imposter.

As if Dr. Holmes's admiration of my work somehow implicated her in the fraud I had perpetrated, I suddenly felt itchy to conclude our awkward meeting at the stationer's and leave. "Are you still teaching Shakespeare?" I asked, trying to sound a bit hurried.

"Actually I'm in my second year of medical school," she said, smiling shyly.

"Was this something you always wanted to do?" I asked.

"My father was a physician," she said, "so a career in medicine was always in the back of my mind. He always considered literature a kind of a diversion, or flirtation. I simply kept putting off the decision until a few years ago when I realized it was now or never. But I honestly don't know if I'll be able to finish." She drew me close, as if the stock clerk searching the shelves for file folders were her dean. "I don't have the mind for it anymore. The memorization is beyond me. I'm too late."

I mumbled a few reassuring words, which graciously she

didn't bother to refute. "I still teach one class at the college and have my old office. Please stop by some time."

I smiled, but knew I wouldn't visit this woman in her sixties still trying to please her father.

"Follow your heart," she had told me. Now, feeling her eyes on me as I left the store and walked up the block, I wondered if she remembered her own words.

XII

"You know how, in the movies, when a person dies or goes to sleep and dreams, a shadowy replica gracefully uncoils from the resting body and begins moving around?" Dr. Marks barely nodded; I had just finished recounting my conversation with Dr. Holmes and had somehow segued into this coda. "That's how I feel about myself sometimes, that there's a weightless woman inside me who escapes every once in a while and I glimpse her out of the corner of my eye. I see her walking, or talking, and think, That's me, that's how I want to be. She has a way of carrying herself — that's the main thing, her posture — that comes from an inner composure I achieve only when I'm alone, only for seconds at a time."

If I were that woman now, I thought, I could just spit out what was on my mind. Instead, I spoke to Dr. Marks as if speech exhausted me. "I always thought that I'd become this woman naturally, by growing older. But now I see that maybe this isn't so. I could get to be Dr. Holmes's age and still worry about what my parents think of me."

I took a deep breath. Dr. Marks was scanning my face, probing my eyes, exquisitely attuned to my words. "When I began to think about coming twice a week," I said, "I kept trying to discover your motives for wanting this, as if my therapy were for you. I didn't know whether you wanted me to go along with you or defy you. I kept trying to come up with a strategy. But now I see that strategy isn't the issue. I want to be that woman

I just described. And I think I want to try coming twice a week."

Until this moment I hadn't given any thought to what kind of reaction I anticipated or desired from Dr. Marks, but I knew that what she did next — smile and dig out her pocket calendar so we could schedule next week's sessions — was perfectly wrong: too understated and at the same time too abrupt.

Instantly I recalled the June evening when I told David that I was going to stay in New York with him rather than move to Colorado to live with the man to whom I had been informally engaged. David's second-floor brownstone apartment happened to be near Central Park, where I was meeting a friend to see an outdoor performance of *Tosca,* and finding the downstairs door open, I walked in without buzzing. Some of my happiest moments of the past year had taken place climbing this very flight of stairs, looking up to see David poised on the landing, one foot keeping his apartment door ajar, patiently and lovingly watching me erase the distance between us.

But that sweltering evening he hadn't been expecting me, although the door to his apartment was half open to capture any stray breeze. Guitar music wafted out to me on the landing; David was sitting, strumming, tilted back in a kitchen chair near the living room's only window, which looked out on the tar roof of a neighboring building, his all-season work boots crossed on the steamer trunk he used as a coffee table.

"I'm staying in New York," I said. David closed his eyes and smiled, but his fingers kept worrying the strings, trying to find an elusive chord for the bridge of the song he was working on. I wondered if he had heard me. It was as if after months of agonizing deliberation I'd decided, OK, what the hell, I'll take this ocean voyage, and I'd packed my things, purchased my ticket, and run down the gangplank only to have David react as if the ship had long ago left port and I'd been aboard all along.

"I mean, I knew he was happy, but he just didn't seem that surprised."

"Maybe he wasn't," Dr. Marks said.

"You weren't either," I said, and she smiled again. Then I remembered a conversation with my brother soon after I began dating David. "How do you feel about him?" my brother had asked. "I don't know," I wailed, "I'm so confused. I love spending time with him, I love taking walks and going shopping with him, I love talking to him, I love the way he cooks, I love his music."

"Sounds like you love him," my brother said.

"It *does*?" I said, wide-eyed.

Dr. Marks chuckled. "You needed someone else to say it out loud before you could say it to yourself."

It seemed so pathetic. No one could accuse me of jumping into things, yet I traveled through life with my foot on the brake, expecting to see a traffic cop materialize in my rearview mirror and ticket me for speeding. Dr. Marks asked me to elaborate.

"Just now," I began, "when you pulled out your calendar, you seemed in such a hurry to schedule my extra appointment next week. It sounds ridiculous, I know."

The same thing had happened with David. When, after a few minutes, I'd said that I had to leave for the opera, he'd hugged me and said, "Guess I'll see you later, then." And I nearly fainted. I had every intention of returning to my apartment that night, for according to the rigid schedule I'd put us on, we didn't have sleep-over dates during the week.

"Why were you on a schedule?" Dr. Marks asked.

"Because I liked him too much," I said; it was all so embarrassing to explain. Seeing David only certain days of the week was supposed to keep my feelings in check and allow me to pay lip service to the commitment with the old boyfriend toward whom my feelings had changed. But my efforts were doomed. David was endlessly accepting toward me. He outlasted my resistance, wore down my objections.

"Yet when he took you up on your decision, you panicked."

Exactly. There was no longer any reason for us not to be together, that night or any night. It had taken me over a year to
accept what I knew in my heart from the first afternoon David
and I spent together, yet that June evening everything felt so
sudden.

"What are you afraid of now?" she asked.

"Taking out my date book and writing down that I'll see you
Tuesday afternoon in addition to Thursday evening."

I'll stay in New York, I'd said to David, as if I were simply
talking about my address and not matrimony; I'll come for therapy twice a week, I said now, as if this meant only a schedule
change. My accessions were a kind of shorthand, because the
terms of the fully executed contract I was signing were frightening for me: yes, I'll take the plunge, though I'm not an expert
swimmer and I panic when I feel out of my depth.

"What's your least favorite part of going swimming?" Dr.
Marks asked.

I smiled — finally, an easy question. "Diving in."

"My therapist and I are going steady now," I joked to my friends
when they asked about my new schedule. "No more casual dating." The romantic metaphor seemed both ironic and apt: I
longed for a token from Dr. Marks signifying the change in our
relationship, something tangible and obvious, something I
could flaunt — a heavy ID bracelet to drape from my wrist in
the manner of a junior high school girl, so long and clunky it
interfered with everything I did, from writing to eating.

Instead all I had was a bad case of postcommitment letdown.
After months of apprehension, coming twice a week to therapy
couldn't have been more anticlimactic. With ninety minutes a
week at my disposal, I went nowhere, the extra time more op-
pressive than liberating, the sessions shapeless, formless, un-
inspired. I stammered and babbled, boring us both.

"I want to try a double session," I announced one day. "I want to be able to talk and not think about the clock." Without a questioning glance, Dr. Marks consulted her date book and penciled me in for back-to-back sessions the following week.

That's when I'd tell her about my summer plans, I promised myself. I'd simply tell her that I wouldn't be able to come to therapy for the next two months, that David and I had decided to spend July and August at his parents' house in the Berkshires. For months I'd postponed this declaration. Already I could visualize the arched eyebrow, the skeptical look, the tone Dr. Marks would use to question me, while keeping her true feelings in check. She'd be furious, and we'd need plenty of time to work this out, I was sure.

But rather than obliterate time, the double session accentuated it. Dr. Marks and I sat facing each other across what felt like a greater distance than usual, boxers in our respective corners, waiting for the start of the round that never came. How dependent I'd become on the rhythm of our snug, forty-five-minute sessions, the good ones unfolding with the inevitability and urgency of a fine short story — exposition, climax, and denouement. With twice as much time I rambled on and on like a third-rate novelist. Worst of all, the issue of my pending summer absence never came up.

An infestation of lice roused me from my therapeutic stupor. Ben had contracted the bugs at day care, and I from him; no one seemed terribly surprised — except me. The diagnosis sickened me. Suddenly ninety minutes of therapy a week wasn't nearly enough time for me to relate the grotesque saga of our delousing: how I had to hold Ben like a football under the kitchen faucet and massage toxic shampoo into his scalp while avoiding his eyes ("Caution," the label read, "excessive exposure can cause brain damage."); how I had to launder everything launderable and vacuum everything else; how I had to disinfect toys and alert everyone we had come into contact with. Then, most odious of all, I had to shampoo four times — my case so advanced, my hair so hospitable to vermin — until I was sure all the insects were flushed out into the basin where I could see them.

"Then," I continued without pausing to wonder how Dr. Marks could stand this, "I had my hair cut. But the nits were still there. So my sister-in-law, who was unlucky enough to be visiting, sat with my head in her lap for hours, sliding louse debris off each shaft of hair — literally nit-picking." Every time I talked about it I felt like fainting and throwing up.

"The only comic relief," I told Dr. Marks, "was in finding out that just about everyone has had a similar episode. Friends told me how they'd had crabs in college, my neighbor once found lice in her eyebrows and eyelashes, and even my mother, that paragon of cleanliness, suffered through a bout with lice when she was fourteen at sleep-away camp." Dr. Marks laughed. For a moment it seemed as if she'd chime in with her own story.

"Lice have nothing to do with cleanliness," Dr. Marks reminded me. I knew that, but it didn't seem to dissipate my disgust. "Exactly what is so upsetting?" Dr. Marks asked, reminding me, as always, that what I took for granted in conversations with myself wasn't immediately apparent to others.

"The sense of profusion, of unchecked proliferation," I said. Dr. Marks nodded as if I'd gotten it exactly right. But suddenly, with the same inscrutable and irrefutable logic present in dreams, this confession led to another.

"I won't be able to come to therapy for July and August," I said, my tone begging for mercy, my body shuddering. I explained my vacation plans. Finally, it had come out, but so childishly, wrapped in my package of Please don't be angry at me, events are beyond my control. But she wasn't angry. She just looked at me, and asked how I felt about not coming to therapy for two months — an aspect of my news which I hadn't considered, perhaps the only aspect. I said that I'd miss it, but my words lacked conviction. I hadn't thought at all about my feelings about missing therapy — only hers. This time, Dr. Marks let me off the hook easily, and simply said that I should call her when I returned to the city after Labor Day. Her voice, free of recrimination and anger, dazed me, but offered me no real relief: I was convinced that she was only pretending not to mind.

Eighteen years a student, six years a teacher — I'd never really outgrown the academic calendar: the end of June marked the end of the year, which started up again in September. Summer was an afterthought, like the handful of leftover milliseconds registering on the atomic clock, belonging neither to the year that was ending nor the one beginning. As a season it had always unnerved me, my clear preference for the regimen of school over the endless lethargy of July and August afternoons making me feel more than slightly heretical.

Walking the long block from the bus stop to Dr. Marks's office, I realized that I was about as nervous facing this last therapy session as I had been for my first, a distant nine months ago.

"So," said Dr. Marks, sitting down and smiling broadly at me. There was no tape recorder. Was this session going to be the therapeutic equivalent of the last day of school, when everyone showed up with nothing left to accomplish — no books to carry, no homework to hand in, nothing to be graded on — only because we had to? I loved catching glimpses of my out-of-uniform teachers — the men in shirtsleeves and the women in sandals, with sunglasses poking out of pockets and handbags; what a shock to realize that they looked forward to summer vacation as much as their students did! Out from behind their desks, without pens and attendance books in their hands, they could have passed for regular adults.

I'd always longed to see Dr. Marks through such an equalizing lens. Today was my best chance, just the kind of chatty, informal session I'd always hoped for. She asked if we were packed for our move to the country, and I asked about her summer plans. But our words sounded flat, one-dimensional, stripped of everything but their face value. We'd emerged from the choppy waters in which we'd been swimming these past months and stood absently on shore, toweling ourselves dry. The very density of the air in her office had changed: it was less fraught with the possibility that anything could happen, that our conversation could surprise us. We were simply two people saying good-bye for the summer. I hated it.

Then I asked if she would be interested in a referral. A friend of my friend Denise was trying to find a therapist.

"Did you already give her my name?" Dr. Marks asked.

"Not yet. Would you be interested?"

"Well, that depends," Dr. Marks said. "How would you feel about my seeing Denise's friend? Do you know her? How close are you? How might it interfere with our relationship?"

I hadn't considered any of this.

"We're not that close," I said. But in fact I had referred to this woman in a recent session. "I suppose it's not the greatest idea."

"I wonder why you asked me about this now," Dr. Marks mused.

"My friend wanted someone good," I said, defensively. I felt terrible that my offer had backfired. It was as if I'd brought a box of chocolates to a friend who was trying to lose weight.

"Maybe you were trying to arrange a trade," Dr. Marks said. "You're leaving, so you offer me your friend."

Soberly, I considered her interpretation. "Are you afraid I'll forget you?" Dr. Marks asked. "Out of sight, out of mind?"

"Maybe," I admitted. "But I can't believe I didn't see this before." Nothing had ever been more transparent.

"You mean you want to be the patient and the therapist. You want to put me out of a job."

We both smiled. Dr. Marks was right. If I could solve my own problems, I wouldn't miss her during my self-imposed absence from her.

Time was running out. A warm breeze billowed the curtains. I wrapped my arms around myself, feeling almost naked. I thought of all the presents for my teacher I had dutifully toted into school on the last day of the year, a bottle of cologne or a lavender sachet my mother had shopped for and wrapped. Today I'd left my house without even my purse, and nothing in my pocket but my bus fare home.

Dr. Marks glanced at the clock and smiled. "Have a good summer," she said, rising.

I hastily stood up too. "You too," I said. I held out my hand and she clasped it in both of hers.

Dr. Marks escorted me to the door, and I took one last look around the room, noticing for the first time a small traveling case, the kind with a separate compartment for a tennis racket, standing near the bookcase. "See you in September," she said. I took a few steps into the corridor and turned back to smile, but she'd already closed her door.

SUMMER

DAVID AND I had our own private downstairs apartment at his parents' country home. In the honeymoon suite, we were not only separated and insulated from the rest of the house, but also temporarily relieved of child care responsibilities by David's parents, who slept upstairs with Ben, woke up with him, fed and dressed him. With the dehumidifier humming, we could hear nothing but footfalls — Ben's energetic steps from bathroom to television, and my mother-in-law's puttering in the kitchen. The room had only one corner window, where the wall met the ceiling; from bed I could glimpse my father-in-law's sneakers as he descended the three porch steps to his car to fetch the daily newspapers. Until he returned — our signal to get up and shower — we were thoroughly sequestered.

It was a comfortable room, if small, containing only a double bed, a dresser, a mirror, and closet, and was in perpetual disarray. We never got around to unpacking our suitcases, which sat gaping on the dresser and the floor. The bed rarely was made, and dirty clothes piled up in the closet; the mail we had forwarded to us was stacked on the plastic night tables. I'd never lived in a room this messy. I was one of the most compulsively neat and clean people I knew, but this summer I seemed to have quite unintentionally slipped out from under the yoke of this compulsion. Something was being undone; I wasn't sure what.

I am sitting on the ground, playing, in the park across from the apartment

*building in which I grew up. My mother sits on a lawn chair, looking
down at me. "When your hair is dirty," she says casually, "it does such
funny things."*

Every night I was visited by such a profusion of dreams that I
felt less asleep than awake in a different medium. Though I'd
suffered from insomnia for years, this summer I fell asleep moments after touching my pillow and spent my nights in a cav-
ernous movie theater where the show never ended. Come
dawn, I'd stumble out into blinding sunlight, aware that the
projector was still running; below the waking words I spoke and
listened to, I could discern the movie's faint soundtrack even
though I couldn't see its images. Never had my dream life felt
so compelling. As I slept downstairs where we couldn't gauge
the light or hear the birds, the night became elastic. I'd wake
some nights after what felt like an eternity of sleeping to see that
it was only one in the morning, that I'd been asleep a mere two
hours, and before I could digest how confusing this was, I fell
asleep yet again.

The sitting room of our suite opened onto a brick patio, and
each morning when I finally roused myself I'd walk outside to
see if the lake was flowing north — our family's barometer of
good weather. The patio would be laced with cobwebs, which
I'd have to bat away, the delicate strands sticking to my hands
and face like the residue of my dreams.

*I need to have surgery again. Suddenly I realize that to have the opera-
tion I'll have to leave Ben. He'll be all alone. I can't wake up; I can't
leave him.*

We spent most afternoons in the car on short excursions through
the Berkshires; Ben would nap, and David and I would sight-
see, sometimes shop. One afternoon my mother-in-law joined
us on a jaunt to West Stockbridge. Ben, who resisted sleep with

as much vehemence as I sought it, woke up cranky. As David and his mother strolled him to the ice cream parlor, I took a slow detour through some jewelry and antiques stores. On the street I passed a familiar face and stopped, my heart palpitating. It was Andrea, not simply a girl I'd gone to school with, but someone who had been as central to my life as anyone I'd known. Tall, almost emaciated, she had her blond hair in the perfect pageboy she'd always worn, the kind I could never achieve, as if she hadn't noticed that the hairdo had gone out of style. For a moment I thought of not approaching her. But then I saw that she had recognized me as well.

In junior high school Andrea exerted what felt like a gravitational pull on me, as if she were a planet and I her smaller, obedient moon. She was "well developed," as we said in those days, and spent her early adolescence caroming from one crush to another — on male teachers, movie stars, television actors. Lacking her ardor, I feared there was something wrong with me, and felt enormously grateful that she tolerated me at all, allowing me to spend time with her in her room, where I could study her trinkets and copy her gyrations, which I did, shamelessly.

Andrea had been the first girl in our circle of friends to lose her virginity, though by that time she wasn't really in our group anymore but only on its outskirts. In fact, when Andrea showed up at my parents' house late one summer night I'd seen very little of her for three years. It was the summer after high school graduation. As if we'd never drifted apart, Andrea grabbed my wrist to lead me to the kitchen table and related a wild story involving the journalism teacher, a man who had served as adviser to the school newspaper, for which Andrea had been editor-in-chief. I couldn't watch her type. Her fingers were long and almost jointless, boneless — monkey fingers. She could bend them in any direction, it seemed, as if they encased nothing hard. Long hairs grew below her knuckles and made her hands look voracious as she gobbled up the keys, one hundred words a minute.

We sat at the kitchen table that night, my mother eavesdropping, I was sure, just outside the doorway. "We made it, finally," Andrea kept repeating. Her clothes were dirty and wrinkled; she said something about not being able to go home, but she didn't ask to sleep at my house and I didn't offer. I was relieved when she left. Our relationship had always been furtive, I realized. Once I mistakenly gave a note intended for her to another friend — this was back in the days when girls wrote notes to each other and folded them into intricate, origami configurations — and was embarrassed for days. And here she was standing before me on the street of a small town in the Berkshires, dressed all in black on a hot summer day, clutching a large styrofoam cup in her long, hairy fingers, and saying how dazzled she was to see me.

She was living in Los Angeles, she said; she'd had a short documentary produced and was working on a new script. She said nothing about a family but grew excited when I mentioned that mine was close by, eating ice cream, and insisted that we join them. She sat down with David and his mother, studied Ben, and told me how lovely he was. I kept having to squelch an urge to say to her, I don't really look like this; usually my hair is longer but I had to cut it because we had lice this spring.

She hadn't kept up with anyone from high school, and as I related gossipy tidbits her eyes glazed over — she really didn't care. I thought I remembered hearing that she had married the teacher — that he'd eventually left his wife and children — but wasn't sure, and didn't ask what had happened. She wasn't wearing a wedding ring or any jewelry at all. We didn't trade addresses or promise to stay in touch. But before we parted she drew me aside and told me how important I had been to her when we were young. She said my friendship had been very precious to her and she had worried that she'd never have the opportunity to thank me.

I didn't know what to say. I'd always assumed that I had received from her more than I had given.

"Not at all," she said. Then she leaned toward me and kissed me, firmly, on my cheek, and walked away.

I drove home that day, regaling David with bits of information about Andrea which suddenly came to mind — that she had been the first person to call for me after we moved into the neighborhood, that her mother had died the year we were in eighth grade, that her father owned a jewelry store and she had a forest of gold- and silver-studded earring trees on her dresser. "She envies you," my mother-in-law said from the back seat where she kept Ben supplied with toys and did her knitting.

"*Envies* me?"

"You're an easy person to envy," my mother-in-law replied, matter-of-factly, implying that I was only pretending not to know this. I kept my eyes on the curving road ahead.

My mother is broke. When I offer to pawn something for her she reacts as if I took too long to make the offer.

When I first met David, I had been in the midst of a seven-year relationship, which had begun the summer after high school graduation. But there was an insidious pattern to my relationship with Michael, which I didn't identify until much too late: no sooner did I accede to one of his many requests — that I transfer colleges to be with him, for example — than he announced that he didn't think we should see so much of each other. After making careful plans to spend a summer together as camp counselors, he decided at the last moment that he had to spend the time by himself, and arranged to work at a different camp only ten miles away from the one he had originally staked out. I was instructed not to be influenced by proximity: he was on retreat and incommunicado until September.

That summer I had a serious accident in a borrowed car. Hit from behind, the car was totaled, and I suffered a severe, legitimate case of whiplash. I was mortified and in terrible pain, but what caused me the most suffering, I think, was trying to decide whether I had sufficient cause to break the code of silence and phone Michael at his camp.

After a week of anguish I placed the call. The moment Michael said hello, I began crying with relief, not caring, in that instant, whether I'd angered him or not.

I told him about the accident and how afraid I'd been to call him. He told me that I'd done the right thing, he understood; I needn't have worried. I sobbed with gratitude.

Everything else was going fine, I assured him, regaining my composure. I had met some great people and was enjoying myself. He told me he was miserable. He missed me.

Could we see each other? He didn't think that would be a good idea. We'll see each other in four more weeks, he said.

It had been the beginning of August, as it was now. I would see Dr. Marks in four weeks and not one day passed when I didn't think of calling her.

David's friend Roger came to visit for a week; recently divorced, he was spending the summer shuttling between friends' country houses, half carrying and half dragging a huge canvas shoulder bag stuffed with all his gear. David and Roger had played music together in college; now they were both graduate students in psychology. They kept in touch only sporadically, but conducted their phone conversations as if they'd spoken just last evening instead of eight or nine months ago, full of present-tense minutiae and virtually no catching up.

Roger needed a place to decompress. From his bulging sack he extracted a huge novel, a beach chair of sorts, sunglasses, and a towel. He parked himself on the deck, a vantage point from which he could observe David and me running after Ben all day, as if we were worker ants.

After lunch Roger would head to the nearby schoolyard to

play tennis or basketball, and would meet us, a few hours later, at the giant supermarket in town where we selected our provisions as if it were a family-operated roadside stand boasting an appetizing array of fresh-picked, fresh-caught fish, vegetables, and fruit. We must have made a strange foursome. I wondered which man people thought I was married to — the one exuding sweat and healthy physical exertion, or the one sweltering with envy and suppressed rage. In the check-out line Ben would demand a brand of cereal or cookie, and after a perfunctory colloquy with me ("I *need* it." "I understand that you want it but we can't buy it.") would collapse on the floor in one of his age-appropriate tantrums. Roger looked as if he wanted to vomit. Eventually we'd carry Ben out of the store and onto the twenty-five-cent horse ride in front of K Mart, negotiating how many turns he could have, enduring yet another tantrum when it was time to leave.

Late one night, after a bottle of wine he drank almost by himself, Roger remarked that he didn't think he had it in him to be a father. "You'd be surprised," David said.

I am talking with my son's pediatrician about the merits of hitting children as a disciplinary method. He argues in favor of it. I say, "Hitting is always a failure of the imagination." But these are not my words; someone else has said them to me.

Around mid-August, Ben's vocabulary and linguistic skills exploded. He'd begun talking soon after his first birthday, but suddenly he was combining words and formulating concepts. Walking near the lake, he saw a stick in the sand and pronounced, "Like a fish." Eating a plate of spaghetti, he said, "Like snakes."

From the moment he was born I'd wondered when I'd be able to have a conversation with him. But how could I have known that a few similes would prove so scintillating?

I'm showing Ben how babies are made. I take one of his dolls and slide it out from under my shirt. "It's easy," I tell him, pushing the doll back into the shade of my clothing, thrusting it out into daylight. He's not sure if he wants to laugh.

In the evening I sometimes watered my father-in-law's flower garden, which grew outside the window of Ben's bedroom. If he heard me, Ben would stand up in his crib and watch me, though we never spoke, as if a wall rather than a screen separated us. Other nights I was alone, watching the rocky soil become wet and fertile. I'm doing all right, I'd think to myself on these evenings, as the sky grew grainy and dark around me. From the lake I heard isolated voices, the rustle of wind, the swish of a canoe nosing its way along the shore. The summers I spent here were as far from a city as I had ever lived. In one week we'd return. The closer I came to seeing Dr. Marks, the farther away she seemed.

The summer after David and I were married we spent an eight-week honeymoon taking the budget version of the grand European tour: England, France, Spain, Italy, Greece, Switzerland, Belgium. Our last stop was Amsterdam, a city I very much wanted to see, but standing in line for tickets to Anne Frank's house I suddenly realized that I couldn't remember the shape and color of the cereal bowls of my dishes at home. I could remember the plates, but not the bowls. That was the moment my vacation ended; I was ready to go home.

Watering the garden that night in late August, I realized that I had no idea what Dr. Marks's summer wardrobe looked like. I missed her, terribly.

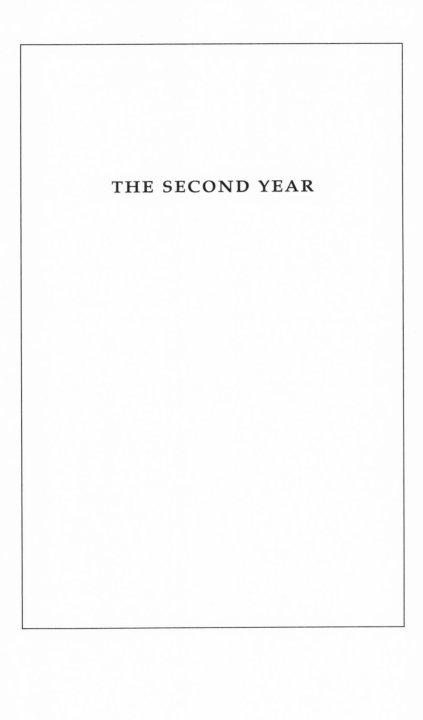

THE SECOND YEAR

I

Dr. Marks looked tanned and rested. We hesitated for a moment before sitting down, grinning, approaching each other with mincing steps like women meeting at a party who want to kiss without messing each other's makeup.

"How was your summer?" I asked, instantly realizing that I didn't much care; rather, I didn't want her reply to take up too much time.

I needn't have worried. She said that it had been fine, that she had gone away for two weeks and then worked, and then she fell silent.

"I had a good summer, too," I began, "and I have so much to tell you about." But it was as if I'd spent the past two months rehearsing a keynote address only to find myself tongue-tied at the podium, my attention snared by a scrap of paper I'd noticed on the floor, or a sudden sound from the back of the room, a detail so trivial yet so absorbing I couldn't begin my speech. For weeks I'd anticipated this moment when I could display the summer's bounty — meeting Andrea, Roger's visit, those dreams — yet tugging at my consciousness with infuriating, inexplicable tenacity was a book I was reading and some minor problems Ben had been experiencing at day care since we returned.

Resisting these distractions, I doggedly returned to my script, reciting in excruciating detail the dreams that had suffused my summer sleep, yet in this room where they should have made sense they sounded utterly senseless. Abandoning them in favor of a new tack, I began describing my meeting with Andrea, but even this juicy anecdote fell flat; my words had no resonance and left Dr. Marks no room in which to react. She looked as trapped and as bored as I was, for as I always advised my writing students, if their own words bored them, their readers would be bored as well.

"So I'm reading this book, a novel, and it bothers me and I don't know why," I resignedly announced to Dr. Marks one day. For the past few weeks therapy had been running like a car whose engine wouldn't kick in: I couldn't get it rolling. What I needed was a jump start, but Dr. Marks, the only motorist who'd stopped, had nothing in the way of tools or jumper cables, and offered only a willingness to stand around with me on the side of the road until real help arrived.

The book I was reading chronicled the psychoanalysis of a young woman who had suffered a severe childhood trauma from which she had never fully recovered. Her case rekindled a set of fears with which I'd long struggled — that I had sought treatment for only the most superficial reasons, that lacking a history and pathology as dramatic or spectacular as the heroine's, my own fledgling twice-a-week therapy was nothing more than an act of supreme self-indulgence.

Actually, a conversation with Roger that summer had also reinforced these fears. One night after dinner Roger and David had started talking about their therapies. I tried to join in, only to have Roger teasingly dismiss my problems as "Oedipal" rather than "pre-Oedipal," as his were. David went on to explain what this meant, but I could barely listen. I had suffered a rebuff. In the hierarchy of problems I came up short.

When Dr. Marks asked me to elaborate, I found I couldn't speak fast enough; in a rush all my impressions of Roger came pouring out. After weeks of trying to force him into the conversation, Roger surfaced effortlessly the moment I relented and allowed myself to talk about what was really on my mind that moment — the book.

"So you feel that Roger and David and the woman in the novel have real reasons for being in therapy," Dr. Marks said.

"Roger goes four times a week, and lies down on a couch. And David tells me he's also tried lying down. And he's thinking of going three times a week." I was barely whispering.

"Do you think about coming three times a week?" Dr. Marks asked.

"Oh God, not again." My twice-a-week schedule still felt stiff and uncomfortable, like a new pair of jeans that needed breaking in. I simply couldn't face the prospect of considering another change.

"You do realize that you're the one who brings up increasing our time," she said.

"I'm just telling you what David said," I answered feebly, for I saw immediately that she was right: I was always responsible for bringing up the subject.

"Do you do analysis?" I asked, hesitantly.

"Sometimes. Do you want to be in psychoanalysis?"

"Do you think I need it?"

"Do you?"

A volley of changing inflections, every question tossed back to me like a tennis ball, but with a spin that made it impossible to return. You tell *me*, I wanted to scream at her. She never answered a question; worse, she was an improviser, an ad-libber, not at all like the analyst in the novel I was reading who had a clear treatment plan in which the effect of each word was expertly calculated, who found herself inexorably drawn to her patient. Countertransference, this was called; Roger and David had given me the term.

"What do you think it would be like to lie down here?" Dr.

Marks asked. Roger had said that it was great to not have to look at your therapist, because then you were freer to speak, to free-associate.

"It would be like speaking into a void," I said softly. I didn't think I could ever do it. I needed to see her face, needed to see her look at me, needed proof that I wasn't simply talking to myself.

"You never ask me about Ben," I said petulantly to Dr. Marks, fully aware that I was beginning the session by spoiling for a fight.

"What should I ask about?" she said.

"How he's doing . . ." my voice trailed off. This wasn't coming out right. I'd begun thinking that I had a legitimate complaint, but after posing one question I was reduced to whining.

"He's having a hard time at day care again," I volunteered finally. Although Ben was with the same teachers he'd had last year, he was again resorting to crying when I left him. From my child development books, I knew that at eighteen months babies reexperience separation anxiety, though Ben seemed more traumatized than anxious, curling one of his arms around mine like a hook and refusing to let go, to be put down, or be transferred into the arms of someone else.

"I know he has to undergo this phase," I said, "but it's so hard on me."

"It should be," Dr. Marks said kindly. "You have to separate from him as much as he does from you." I let that thought sink in, realizing that I finally felt free to not speak, to not react to everything she said. "What does his teacher say? Does the staff have any suggestions?" Dr. Marks seemed involved in the discussion now, as if she hadn't noticed that I'd raised the subject merely to get a rise out of her, or else she didn't care. She was taking me at my word, I suddenly realized; she was surprisingly trusting.

"His teacher suggested that he bring in a favorite toy from home. Like a stuffed animal." I'd selected one, actually, since Ben had shown no preference — a beautiful panda, a gift from my brother, with a lustrous coat of black and white fur. Minnie, Ben had named her, after Benjaminnie, I supposed. And the presence of this bear did calm him. He clutched it after I left, the teacher told me, until he felt ready to leave it behind in the soft corner and meet the day. "I think things like this are called transition objects," I said.

Dr. Marks seemed unimpressed by my erudition; that I could speak her language meant nothing to her, I saw with chagrin. "Did you have a Minnie when you were growing up?" Dr. Marks asked.

I recalled a white stuffed musical elephant whom I called Bob, but he wasn't the first; my mother tells me that when I was a baby I had a cloth doll I called Kono.

"What happened to Kono?" Dr. Marks asked.

I had no idea. I assumed that after a certain point the relationship was discouraged and she faded from prominence.

When Dr. Marks asked what gave me that impression I had my answer all ready: my parents, with their rather rigid time-table of child development, wouldn't have tolerated my dragging a toy around with me for very long. They were nonplussed that I sucked my thumb as long as I did.

"How long?" Dr. Marks asked.

I had been about ten when I finally stopped, old enough to remember the exact conversation that cured me. My pediatrician, in cahoots with my parents, graphically described how the germs from an infection on my middle finger would travel across to my thumb and down into my stomach unless I stopped.

Dr. Marks smiled. My parents had also weaned my brother from milk bottle to cup by telling him that his bottle had broken when in fact they'd hidden it in the never-touched liquor cabinet. Years later my brother found the bottle; incensed, he confronted our parents, who couldn't believe that he felt as betrayed as he acted.

We had both been betrayed, lied to by people who in most arenas were more scrupulous than anyone we knew. They paid their income tax down to the penny, returned money to cashiers who carelessly undercharged them — to use the word *dishonest* in the same sentence with either of my parents seemed unthinkable.

Yet about their feelings my parents lied all the time. Said they weren't angry when they were. Hid bottles they claimed were broken.

"And I'm just the same way," I said. "I may know when I'm lying but I go ahead and do it anyway. I'd always much rather tell a lie than an unpleasant truth. I can't even begin to calculate how many times a day I lie."

The admission roused the scathing voice inside me, the reprimand of a person who loathed me, who greeted my confession with a deserved dose of recrimination. But this time I knew better than to think that it came from Dr. Marks, and instead of shying away from her gaze I looked hopefully at her with the same look I'd seen so often on Ben's face when he wanted me to rescue him. *Rescue me,* I implored her; tell me where this voice is coming from; make it stop. It's not simply the case that I lie and I am therefore a reprehensible person, is it?

"What were they afraid of, do you think?" Dr. Marks asked.

Afraid of?

"Often people who lie are afraid of the truth," Dr. Marks explained in a measured tone.

"Afraid of their feelings," I ventured. Afraid that if people spoke their minds there would be reprisals, explosions, collapses. "And I don't want Ben to feel this way, I can't stand it, it's like living in a pressure cooker, it's so hypocritical."

And suddenly I was in tears, groping for one of the boxes of tissues Dr. Marks had strategically placed around the room. I allowed myself to sit and cry, closing my eyes, letting my tears flow, aware that Dr. Marks had nothing to do but sit and watch me and wait for me to finish, but somehow at peace with this knowledge. Sure enough, when I was spent, I found her looking at me kindly, waiting for me to resume.

"I suppose I could use a Minnie now too," I said, smiling. With a start I suddenly remembered the birth dream I had had over the summer — it had been Minnie, not an anonymous doll, that I kept pulling out of my shirt.

"I wonder who was being born in that dream," Dr. Marks asked. I smiled, as if her question had been merely clever, and I began recalling the night of Ben's birth. My labor had been as terrifying and relentless as a whirlpool threatening to suck me into oblivion. Adrift on a private ocean I tried to resist the tide, but there was no going back to shore, no end to the pain drowning my senses. The desperate pushing, the abandoned shrieking — *was that me?* — echoing off every metal surface in the sterile, steel room, and then he was out and with his arrival came relief, *relief* unequaled by any other.

"I didn't take any medication," I bragged, for I was proud of my fortitude, "so I was not only awake for every second of it, but I also felt as if I'd never been more aware. It was the most extraordinary moment of my life."

I stopped short. Dr. Marks had never had any children. Was it upsetting her to hear me talk like this? She didn't look upset. She looked interested. I continued, unable to stop now, just as I had been unable to stop the birth.

The first moment I had seen Ben he was such a squirmy, wet, slimy thing, yet every cell in my body strained toward him, claiming him; he was mine. The nurses were anxious to whisk him away to clean him and swaddle him up, but I memorized him in that first moment, gunk and all. It wasn't exactly love at first sight; I didn't "love" him in the way I expected until months later, with the dawn of his consciousness. But the very word *love* seemed so puny for what I was feeling that first moment when we bonded, or imprinted, or whatever they call it, when I memorized him and he me, for he was already on my stomach, skin to skin, sucking me. It felt deeper than love, a feeling I hadn't known about until that moment, part protection and part relief and part gratitude and part wonder. It was raw and new, fierce, primal — a kind of indisputable recognition — I know you, you are of me.

I paused, glanced up almost abashedly for having run on so long. *Yes? . . .* Dr. Marks's perfectly composed glance seemed to be saying, *Go on.*

I began telling her about the afterbirth, the placenta, which slid out of me when I wasn't looking, a bloody knot of tissue that landed in a bucket at the doctor's feet. The doctor asked David if he wanted to see it; it had to be inspected. I looked too. It was liverish, almost surreally disgusting, so revolting it was compelling. It couldn't possibly have come out of me. Someone, the doctor or David, I didn't remember who, said that in some cultures this was considered a delicacy. Suddenly I wanted to touch it, to squeeze it. This is what had nourished my baby; I created this, or it was created inside me.

"The placenta wasn't in my dream," I hastily explained to Dr. Marks. She smiled and I instantly realized that the dream wasn't simply a demonstration and it wasn't simply about Ben. In it I was giving birth not only to my son but to myself. I looked up, astonished.

"And the placenta is like my feelings," I said, sure that Dr. Marks knew exactly what I was talking about. Both ugly enough to want to spurn, impossible to renounce, they were mine, perfectly intact, as the doctor had told me, only I couldn't throw them out, not ever. In fact they were sitting here in a bucket at my feet, in this office, with this woman who was suddenly more midwife than therapist, as therapy became a disembodied, mysterious birthing process all its own.

II

FOR CHANUKAH we gathered at my parents' house — my brother and his fiancée, David, Ben, and I. As she cleared the table before dessert, my mother casually mentioned that her gynecologist had found a lump in her breast, and that she was slated for a mammogram in three days.

I clutched a napkin in my hand and ran out of the kitchen toward my old bedroom, where I threw myself on my bed.

My father came in first, standing near me with his arms akimbo. He never knew what to say at junctures like these. I could recall many other times when I was sick or upset and he came in wanting to help, not knowing what to do, usually resorting to a joke, which I was never in the mood for but felt obliged to smile at. "What's up?" he asked. Was he kidding? Did he genuinely not know? Did he want me to say aloud what he couldn't? Did I have to explain that situations that began as innocuously as this sometimes ended badly — as my cousin Lily's had? Or was his question a kind of code, a way of coaxing me to pull myself together?

"You sound angry," David once observed to my father, surprised that an innocuous conversation had taken a disputatious turn. Fists clenched, face red, my father said, "I'm not angry." I recalled this incident as I returned to the table, the scene of my outburst. It was clear that everyone had been talking about me. I felt like my grandmother, who always made a nuisance of herself in public places, complaining that the soup was too cold or the bathroom unclean, while the rest of us picked at our food and tried to pretend we didn't know her.

Both my parents insisted that Ted not come up for my mother's "procedure," adding that I needn't change my plans, either. But that morning I woke up knowing that I wanted to be with them, so I entrusted Ben to a friend, who would bring him to day care, and took the train and a cab to my parents' house. "I would have picked you up," my father exclaimed when he opened the door. That I'd come didn't seem to surprise him; what flustered him was that I hadn't called and asked for a ride home from the station. I'd meant to be considerate; it had never dawned on me that he might need something to do, that having foreclosed on his opportunity to ferry me home was in effect tightening the knot around his hands, presenting him with one more scenario in which he was helpless.

I tried to ascertain what arrangements had been made — whether the surgeon had procured permission to perform anything more than a lumpectomy — but my father was vague about which papers, if any, had been signed. He seemed surprised that I'd brought it up, as if I'd recklessly broken an unspoken pact to keep our conversation free of the contagion that the mention of doctors, disease, or complications would bring. Call the hospital, I suggested, find out what's going on. But he was paralyzed. When I volunteered to call he refused my help: he'd been asked to wait, and so he waited.

"Like a child," I had told Dr. Marks earlier that week. "Both my parents are behaving like children." When she asked me to explain, I was brimming with examples of their passivity: their inability to question the doctors, their reluctance to switch to doctors affiliated with a more reputable hospital. Their reaction to friends and relatives who wished to help or simply to express concern was subdued and tinged with faint rejection, but this didn't surprise me; their response to any kind of family difficulty was to circle the wagons and keep mum. But I'd never known them to practice denial so extensively, to act so meekly in the face of imminent and real catastrophe. "They think good patients don't peep, and by not peeping they'll be rewarded with a good prognosis."

I'd seen glimpses of this reaction before. Just a few days after Ben's birth, when he had to be admitted to the hospital with acute neonatal jaundice, and his bilirubin count was spiraling higher, and the doctors were muttering words like "complete blood transfusion," I stumbled to a phone and called my parents. Bring him here, my mother suggested — meaning to her neighborhood, to the now elderly general practitioner who had been my doctor, to their local hospital. Bleeding from every major artery, I'd looked to my parents for support, only to have them instruct me to drink the blood of two chickens whose necks I'd broken — a voodoo cure.

Dr. Marks laughed. "What did you want them to say?" she asked. I paused. I'd never thought about it.

"I wanted them to extricate me from the situation, to make it all better. And I wanted them to tell me that I was doing the right thing, that my judgment was good. I mean, we'd brought our son to the attention of the head of pediatrics of one of the best hospitals in the entire country — not bad for two new and very crazy parents."

"So you want them to treat your mother's illness as you treated your son's."

"Well, where do they get off telling me what to do and meanwhile they don't know the first thing about how to get information from doctors."

"Unless they don't want to get information," Dr. Marks said.

That's impossible, I felt like saying. Impossible, because that position wasn't reasonable. It wasn't logical. And these were the qualities most prized by my parents, especially by my father, who was now in charge.

"Maybe he feels overwhelmed," Dr. Marks said. But how

could he feel that way after devoting his life to moderation, to reason, to logic? Those were the qualities he instilled in me; that's how I knew how best to handle this crisis. How could he not know too? How could he betray me, desert me?

"A friend of mine called last week," I said. "A friend whose father died of cancer two years ago. And when I told him about my mother he said, 'Get a pencil and copy down these numbers,' and he rattled off the numbers of Cancer Care and five other self-help groups. And I pretended that I was copying them down because mostly I was furious at him. I mean, I know he meant well, but I wasn't ready to hear that my mother has cancer."

"Maybe that's how your parents feel," Dr. Marks said.

I shot her a black look; was she taking their side?

"I wonder why you want your parents to change," she mused, "why you need them to be different. This is probably a bad time to expect it from them."

"This is a perfect time," I insisted. "Exactly the right time to marshal their resources and rise to the occasion."

"Why do you need them to be different?" she persisted.

"Then I could be, too," I said, meekly.

"Can you change without changing them?"

"That would be a betrayal."

"But you just said they're betraying you."

"My mother didn't mean to get sick," I said, near tears, "it's not her fault. I should be more sympathetic. Sometimes I think I would have more feelings for just about anyone else who was sick, a friend, even a perfect stranger . . ."

I cried quietly for a few minutes. "I guess that's the point. They're not anyone else, they're my parents. When I used to think about them dying, I'd say to myself, 'If my mother dies, if my father dies, I'll go crazy.' But it's not 'if,' it's 'when.' "

I looked up. Dr. Marks was gazing at me very intently and nodding her head. Well, say something, I wanted to scream at her, contradict me, *comfort* me. The seconds of her silence ticked away — for once we'd both run out of words.

I recalled the details of this session walking from room to room at my parents' house, checking the table on which my mother displayed new issues of the magazines she and my father subscribed to, the blotter of her desk for letters she'd recently received, her desk drawer for new pens, the message board near the telephone. As I snooped around I realized that this was no random check but a ritualized search I always performed soon after arriving, to sniff out changes, to reclaim the part of the house that was mine from the time when I had lived here.

The house was in perfect order; nothing would have betrayed the fact that my family was undergoing an upheaval, except my father's presence at home in the middle of a working day, pacing the house in slow motion, from den to bathroom and back. During one trip he stuck his head in my room, where I sat on my bed, and suggested that maybe this would be a good time to clean out my closet.

"Today?" My mother had long wanted me to go through the boxes I had stowed there, but now? In the midst of her operation? "It can wait," I said, but when I looked up I saw disappointment in my father's eyes. Had this been some kind of message?

The last time I remembered being alone with my father like this was the day before I was married, when we found ourselves lunching together in a house abuzz with activity. Outside, workmen were erecting the tent for the next day's festivities, doors slammed, phones rang, and from my father's expression I knew he'd envisioned a more formal and more serene setting for the conversation he was about to embark upon. Accepting, however, that this was probably our last private moment, he began by describing the scene that greeted him every Friday night when he came home to find a spotless house and a formal dinner, prepared and lovingly served by my mother, ready for him right here, in the dining room. "It's so, so lovely," he said, and tears came to his eyes.

I nodded, touched and slightly amused — a paean to a clean and orderly house wasn't what I had expected in the way of prenuptial advice — and waited for him to get to the point. But it seemed he was finished. With a kiss to my forehead he left me open-mouthed at the table.

That he was instructing me I knew, but to do what? Keep a clean house? Observe the Sabbath? Cook? His shorthand was elliptical, evasive: you must understand me, his exhortations always implied, because I won't spell things out for you. So much of my family education had been in this mold — unstated, enigmatic, inscrutable. We loved each other — this was never in question — but there were so many other feelings we couldn't broach with each other.

I opened the door to my closet. Sagging on their hangers were the black velvet dress I'd worn to my first dinner party when I was eighteen; a velour bathrobe I no longer fit into; and a fox stole, its tiny eye gaping at me from beneath mangy fur — one of the few things my mother salvaged from her mother's apartment before calling in Goodwill. In the boxes piled on the shelves and floor were an old boyfriend's lock of hair wrapped in blue tissue paper, rocks and shells collected from the private beach where I had trespassed the day after high school graduation, diaries, letters, mementos, keepsakes — the detritus of my emotional life, the archive of my sentimental education, each item evoking a palette of feelings I had no words for, and so had to keep hidden. From an ugly orange poncho I'd sewn for myself before going off to college I extracted a long hair that had been buried in the weave since high school. I could no sooner dispose of these possessions than eat them.

My father was in the kitchen sitting at the table, drumming his fingers on the tabletop. I'd never seen him idle for so long.

"Look," I said suddenly, "let me make you some coffee. Would you like some?"

He hesitated. Moments passed. His face clouded up. Yes, no, what was the right answer? He wasn't sure. My mother wasn't there. Did I want some? He looked at me angrily as if I were responsible for his confusion.

Just say yes or no, I wanted to tell him, but to say that to someone like my father was like saying to the insomniac, "Just close your eyes and relax," or to the hypochondriac, "That palpitation is all in your head." A neurosis, I realized, is something that can't be conquered by will power.

I sat down at the table across from my father, roughly the same distance from him as Dr. Marks sat from me, and settled into her pose, leaning back, feet up, relaxed yet intense. Dr. Marks wouldn't force him to speak. Instead she'd listen to his silence, read the tightness in his hands and his throat. Who would speak first? Who would succumb?

An interesting word, Dr. Marks would remark, *succumb*. What did I mean? Was talking a form of giving in? Was silence power? Were these silent struggles all struggles for control?

How did she do it? How had she insinuated herself into my parents' house? How had she maneuvered herself so that I found myself talking to her all day? How had she crawled under my skin and into the part of my mind that spoke to itself so that I could carry on a running conversation with her in this bastion of reserve? I didn't love her; I didn't know her, yet I was attached to her. In her presence I was received in ways that I could never be received around this table where I was both loved and cherished.

"What do you want to say to your father?" I imagined Dr. Marks asking next. And for the first time I heard the magic word in that sentence — *want* — not should, but want. What I wanted to say, to shout, to cry, was simply, Talk to me. Talk. You must have so much on your mind. What word do you need to hear to unlock your thoughts?

"Is it your job to supply the missing word?" Dr. Marks might ask.

But he looks so completely ill at ease, what else can I feel but a desire to ease his discomfort?

I saw Dr. Marks lean forward in her seat, ready to pounce. Wait, she'd say, listen to yourself. But I'd already heard it. He feels bad, I have to make him feel better; if *a*, then *b*, with the irrefutable logic of a mathematical proof. But there was no natural, logical bridge from the first statement to the second, just the long and burdensome weight of tradition, of ritual, of habit. Maybe I didn't have to make him feel better — obviously I couldn't. Even the offer of a cup of coffee brought with it more consternation than comfort.

"What's in the bag?" my mother asked. She was sitting up in bed, answering all calls herself, deflecting questions about how she was feeling. The procedure had been uneventful, and although the mass had looked benign, the pathology report would take several days. My parents seemed completely relieved, whereas I still felt enormously agitated.

I'd been shopping, I told her, at the suburban mall where I'd spent a good part of my adolescence. One of David's cousins was getting married next month and I'd become completely obsessed with my appearance, as if movie producers were to be among the invited guests. For this party, I'd shopped for a new dress, bought a new perfume, and scheduled the first manicure of my life — for what effect I wasn't sure; only aunts and uncles and cousins I'd seen dozens of times before would be there.

My mother looked at me skeptically. What are you supposed to do the day your mother has breast surgery? I wondered.

"I have to go now," I said. "I have to get Ben." But that wasn't true. David was going to pick up Ben.

"Don't come visit again, don't come home this weekend; I'll be fine." My mother's parting instructions.

She wants to deprive herself, Dr. Marks would say.

"It's as if they're both prisoners," I said, collapsing onto the couch in Dr. Marks's office when seven o'clock finally came around. "And the worst part is that I am too. I can't open up either; what I hate in them I hate in myself."

"Maybe you're ready to organize a prison break," Dr. Marks said. Her words caught me off guard. I laughed to think of myself behind bars, banging with a spoon to let us out. But no, it wouldn't be like that. Instead I saw myself scheming quietly in a cell the size of my closet, careful to attract no undue attention, for in the end I'd have to go it alone.

III

FROM BEHIND A CLOSED DOOR I heard a telephone ring until an answering machine clicked on, then a woman's voice talking into a tape. I looked at my watch; whether I was arriving for my evening or afternoon session I was always early. Once a week I arrived at dusk, the food stains on my sweatshirt testifying to the long, hard day I'd put in playing Mom; for my other appointment I arrived fresh from work in a skirt and silk blouse and toting a briefcase bulging with compositions, memos, and textbooks — the ballast of my professional life.

I no longer met Dr. Marks at the Institute but at a new office in a ground-floor suite. The waiting room was stocked with recent magazines and sported a few pale paintings. In one corner sat a machine emitting white noise, as if to drown out conversation, but there was none. When a second phone began ringing it ran on forlornly for what seemed like minutes.

A door opened and I heard footsteps down the hall. To see Dr. Marks and her client I would have had to crane my neck and deliberately peer around the corner. The front door of the suite opened and closed. Dr. Marks walked briskly back down the narrow corridor and into the bathroom adjoining her office. I heard a flush, then I heard her door close: she was back in her office. What did she do? Make some phone calls? Review my case? Have a drink? Look out the window? I tracked her like a hunter.

In the tiny, dingy bathroom in the suite's entryway, I peered into the medicine cabinet mirror to apply new rouge, mascara, lipstick, primping for therapy as if I were auditioning for a play, and I remembered the dream I had had the night before: *I am in the operating room. The surgeon stares at my abdomen before slicing it open and says, "This will be a minor repair," as if I have some structural fault, or a leak. And I think, Oh God, I don't have any makeup on.*

At exactly four-thirty Dr. Marks opened her office door and came to fetch me. I'd had time to begin grading my papers, and greeted her with a smile that said, So soon? She stood waiting for me as I gathered my things — my papers, pens, marking book, newspaper — and rose to follow her down the hallway, which in its narrowness reminded me of a gangplank.

In Dr. Marks's office I flopped onto the couch, put down my papers and my briefcase, looked around, plumped a pillow and settled it in the small of my back — a "Honey, I'm home" interlude. I checked to see what Dr. Marks was wearing, and if she had bought the newspaper that day. This was a much smaller room than the one at the Institute; from my seat I could read the titles in the bookcase on the opposite wall.

"How do you feel about the change in address?" Dr. Marks had asked a few weeks before. I liked it. "Some clients find it a bit disorienting at first," she prompted me, knowing that I sometimes needed a spur, but this time I wasn't holding back — I felt genuinely comfortable here. I felt as I did when David and I shed the roommates we had been living with and rented an apartment alone together, where our furniture consisted of a mattress on the bedroom floor, some borrowed bamboo chairs and a coffee table in the living room, and a huge, ungainly mahogany dining table, a castoff from David's mother's hairdresser, in the luxurious third room whose purpose we hadn't yet specified.

We'd known each other only a year, David and I, when we'd taken up housekeeping, a phrase from my mother's generation.

The apartment embodied a paradox: a material manifestation of our commitment to each other, it nonetheless transcended the material. And that's how I felt about Dr. Marks's new office. I knew that she saw other patients here, that other people sat on this couch, perhaps in the same spot I claimed as mine, talked to her, listened to her, had their names listed in her phone book, paid her. But I didn't think about them. Coming twice a week to therapy had made it a phenomenon both more and less abstract. Sitting in this room for a circumscribed period of time was as much a part of my routine as brushing my teeth, yet what therapy seemed to be about had less and less to do with place or time; if anything, it seemed a way of thinking, of talking — to Dr. Marks, to myself — a method of paying attention to certain details or nuances in tones of voice which would otherwise escape detection. Therapy was acquiring its own distinctive atmosphere; conversation that sprouted here would wilt elsewhere.

I had long ago stopped preparing brilliant opening salvos; one of the fringe benefits of coming twice a week was that I allowed myself to begin talking wherever I found myself. "You know, I just spent five minutes in the bathroom putting on new mascara, which I'm going to forget about, and when I rub my eyes I'll end up looking like a raccoon."

Dr. Marks, prepared to follow me into whatever humdrum corners I should wander, said, "I wonder if this is related to your concerns about the wedding next month." Unfailingly riveted to me, she worked like a novelist, like a lover, remembering shards of distant conversations, piecing disjointed thoughts together with invisible threads of attentiveness.

"I was never interested in cosmetics before," I said, wondering where in the world this conversation would meander. I didn't push. We were teasing at the subject matter. "It wasn't politically correct to use makeup or shave your legs or admit that you cared about how you looked when I was in college. I still don't wear makeup when I see certain friends. They'd take it the wrong way."

"Which way is that?" she asked quickly.

"You know, like I'm being frivolous, vain, caring more about what's on the surface than underneath . . ." I trailed off, staring at Dr. Marks's manicured, polished fingernails, her eye shadow, her lipstick, her coiffed hair.

"Maybe these days you feel more comfortable thinking about what's on the surface than what's underneath," Dr. Marks said.

I didn't respond to that; instead, I painted a tableau: my mother standing at her dresser in front of her mirror, dabbing on rouge, dotting perfume behind her ears, blotting her lipstick with tissue that she kept in her top drawer, the drawer that smelled of face powder and nail polish, the only drawer in the entire house that wasn't neat.

"My mother doesn't wear much makeup now," I added.

"Does that mean that you can't, either?" Dr. Marks asked.

"But why do I care so much? I never used to. I mean, I cared when I was in high school. Then we had fights about what I could and couldn't put on my face all the time. My parents were very rigid."

"Sounds like your friends are too," Dr. Marks said.

"But if you could see me, if you knew how much time I waste debating whether or not I should have a pedicure, how many hours I spend tending to the cuticles on my toenails. I don't even have any open-toed shoes, why should I care what my damn feet look like?"

The mockery, the derision in my tone hung in the air like breath on a cold morning, as palpable as a specimen zipped into a naturalist's plastic bag. I was sitting on her couch with my feet curled up beside me, running my fingers over my toes, my arches, begging her to tell me how loathsome I was, how petty, how pathetic, how vain — tell me, and I'll believe you. Just tell me.

But of course she didn't. "It sounds as if what makes you most uncomfortable is trying for something you want. That you have to *work* at looking the way you want to look is troublesome. Think of the word itself, 'makeup.' I think that you're hesitant to make things up, to try to create something, whether it be your face and your toes for a party, or yourself."

"Does everything always have to stand for something?" I asked, weakly, knowing even as I whined that the answer was No, not always, but now, in this case, yes. If only I were talking only about cosmetics. But I seemed to have a peculiar knack for imbuing even the most trivial object — a vial of lipstick — with psychic weight. Nothing in this subdued beige office was neutral or out-of-bounds; no object was too minuscule to be the subject of our attention; nothing I thought about was free from the taint, the idiosyncratic stamp, of me.

"I hate standing in front of the mirror. I get shaky and frustrated. I'm terrible with colors, I don't know what looks good on me, I can't put the stuff on right."

"Can you practice?" Dr. Marks asked. "Can you have a makeup consultation?"

"I can't afford it," I said. This was what I always said whenever the subject of my coming to therapy three times a week came up.

"What happens if you try?" Dr. Marks persisted.

"If you have to try for something it's ruined." With that I felt myself sliding into the spongy, faintly repellent, regular, unoutstanding, uneventful past. Ashamed of its paltriness, I began relating an incident from sixth grade when I wasn't chosen to be in a gymnastic competition. My teacher told me that she didn't think I could do twenty-five push-ups. I told her I could. She granted me a week to practice. I did. A week later I could do thirty. I was in the show.

More: I moved when I was in seventh grade, and at the end of my first day at the new school everyone in my homeroom received report cards. One girl was singled out for teasing —

"Did you get all A's, Jane?" everyone taunted. Next time they'll be asking me, I promised myself.

"And they did," I told Dr. Marks. "Two months later I had the best report card in the class. That was important to me, and I did it. I did it." I was in tears: what an admission, that I had coveted something as meaningless as grades, that I had put myself in competition, that this was indeed the last time in my memory that I could remember consciously going after something I wanted. "That's pathetic," I said, dabbing at my eyes, mascara running, feeling a complete mess. "I don't know how to say 'I want,' " I sobbed. "It was taken out of my vocabulary."

"Maybe Ben can help you learn how," she said.

I stopped short. We'd spent both sessions last week discussing an incident at day care when Ben had first pulled the blond hair of, and then sunk his teeth into, the arm of his friend Julie.

Beyond mortification, I had wanted nothing to do with Ben; I recoiled from him. When he clung to me, when he reached for my hand as we walked home together, I very nearly hated him.

"Children go to the heart of their feelings," Dr. Marks had said. "They aren't interested in making nice or forcing smiles."

"I try to give him other options when he gets angry," I said. "Hit pillows, shout, stamp your feet —"

"He's only two," she said.

" 'I *want* it, I *need* it,' " I said in his imploring voice.

She smiled. "You sound envious."

I blushed with embarrassment, anger, and bafflement. "Of what?"

"You tell me," Dr. Marks said.

But I couldn't. I didn't have a clue. "His day care teacher told me to stay with him, whatever that means. She said I should blot out everything else — what I thought the other parents were feeling, what I felt, and just think of what he was feeling. 'Go with him, be with him,' she said. Where the hell am I if not with him, twenty-four hours a day?"

"You're with him physically," Dr. Marks had said, staying

calm in the face of my scorn and bitterness. And it had taken me two weeks to understand the point she was making: I had in fact distanced myself from him. I couldn't cozy up to the part of him that felt angry enough to bite. I couldn't accept the part of me that wanted things — especially something as frivolous as a pedicure.

"In other words," I said slowly, "I have to learn how to be a two-year-old again."

"Maybe not again," Dr. Marks said. "Maybe for the first time."

I am invited to a literary cocktail party, but at the last minute I leave the room and go upstairs on a balcony to dine with the children. I look down on the gathering I long to be in the midst of.

"Where do you belong?" Dr. Marks asked when I related this dream. "With the adults or with the children?"

I go to see Ben's pediatrician, whose office is in the medical office of the college I attended. No one is there; I snoop around, poke into confidential files while I wait for him. He calls much later, and by then I am furious, but he says that he is sick, his whole family is sick; he has to meet me on a street corner. There he tells me how much he needs me and loves me, that no one understands him as I do. We go to his apartment where his wife is making something in the blender; his mother and son sit at the table. The grandmother remarks that her grandson pales beside my son.

"Why am I dreaming about my son's pediatrician?" I asked her.

"Tell me about him," she said, as if she wanted nothing more than to listen.

"There are three doctors," I began, "all young, and I have crushes on them, especially one. He's not even attractive — he's overweight and at times can be pretty condescending — but I find myself walking down the block to an appointment feeling as if I were going on a date. I just feel very attached to him; he's so intimately connected to Ben, to Ben's health and well-being, I need him so much, need his advice, his guidance, his approval that I'm doing a good job of mothering. I'd go all the time if I could.

"But I don't think it's that unusual," I added defensively. "Many women have told me that they've developed crushes on their child's pediatrician. One of my friends didn't even realize how dressed up she had gotten for an appointment until the doctor said to her, 'Are you going to a party?' "

Dr. Marks laughed with me, but I saw that she wasn't deterred. The fact of other women's crushes wasn't an issue here, only mine.

My son's pediatrician is my gynecologist. I wait and wait in a hospital lounge, his waiting room, which is packed. I need to pee but don't want to miss my turn. I finally find the bathroom but can't urinate. Moments later my name is called — I am the last patient — but when I enter the examining room his wife is there. A big plastic container falls from a top shelf and I am able to catch it. Then we all leave together.

"What about this dream disturbs you?" Dr. Marks asked as she watched me fidget during the telling. Even I heard how close my voice was to a whisper.

"I don't like dreams when I dream about peeing. I'm frantic that I will. I used to, when I was a kid."

"What about it troubles you?"

My first reaction to these questions was still an angry "Is she dense?" To think that she didn't understand why the thought of wetting myself plunged me into the depths of humiliation seemed impossible, her modulated response more a ploy to get me talking than a genuine feeling. But maybe it would be helpful for me to put my unspoken dread into words.

I told her about the times I remembered wetting my bed as a child. My parents were always disappointed, but their reaction was muted — I didn't remember any scenes of horror and shame. But the shame lived within me to that moment. In fact, I couldn't believe that I was telling her about it. To clam up, though, seemed greater foolishness.

"What do you think these dreams are about?" she asked.

"I don't know, what do you think?" I asked her point-blank, a new tactic.

"Well, I'm not sure. Enuresis is sometimes a reaction to undue pressure, or anger, or a kind of release. I'm not sure yet what it means to you. But I think they are all therapy dreams, dreams about therapy."

I nodded as if to say, Of course, I knew that, but of course I didn't. Therapy dreams? Don't flatter yourself, I told her, silently.

I am running in a race across a huge expanse of sand; the goal is a wall of buildings looming ahead of me, like hotels at a seaside resort. I am running well, but then I see someone or something to my right and run toward it on a diagonal course. I lose the race. My coach, a woman, severely reprimands me.

"I just wanted to remind you," I said as we began a session in mid-June, "that I won't be coming to therapy this summer." If Dr. Marks was surprised she didn't show it. In truth, this was no reminder; last year when I made an identical announcement I'd given her no hint that the summer pilgrimage to the Berkshires was an annual event. Nonetheless, I slurred through my prepared statement as if she had been expecting it. If anything, I was even more nervous than last year since I'd postponed telling her until nearly the last moment.

"I think the break will be good for me," I went on. The idea of coming to therapy three times a week kept cropping up with frightening regularity, particularly after the several double sessions we'd had to schedule recently. Ninety uninterrupted minutes of therapy seemed to work on me the same way an evening

of drinking in the local student pub had when I was in college —
loosening my tongue and my inhibitions. "I wish our regular
sessions could be like this," I would say as I roused myself out
of a not unpleasant stupor. I liked feeling too tired to care what
I was saying, as if the reproving part of my mind had shorted
out through overuse. Then Dr. Marks would ask me what I
thought about coming to therapy more often. And I always
snapped that I couldn't afford it — as if it were Dr. Marks's
fault.

We'd been through this script before when I was deciding
whether or not to come to therapy twice a week instead of once.
Had I made no progress at all? Yet if it was progress I wanted,
all I had to do was agree to come more often. But I couldn't. I
remembered how it felt to stand on the beach, feet in the wet
sand, waves breaking around my ankles, the tug of the increasingly insistent current burying my feet deeper and deeper until
moving from that spot became unimaginable.

"I was going to bring you flowers," I said to Dr. Marks, settling
empty-handed into my last appointment of the summer before
my vacation.

"Last year you wanted to bring me a new client," Dr. Marks
said, faintly smiling.

"I remember. That's partially why I didn't bring a present this
time; I didn't want to offer a bribe." I paused. "And I also
figured, since you said you were going away next week anyway,
that you wouldn't even be here to see them."

"Or you," she said.

I looked at her, puzzled.

"You won't be here either," she said.

"Or me," I parroted. Nearly six weeks would pass before I'd
understand the sense she made out of my aborted gesture: even
if I wasn't going to be here, she had her nerve leaving me.

THE THIRD YEAR

I

THE PHONE RANG seven or eight times. Just as I despaired of ever hearing her voice again, Dr. Marks's answering machine clicked on, her cadence exactly as I had remembered it. So she was still here after all, had been here in my absence tending to her other clients who hadn't taken so protracted a summer vacation. "I'm back," I said onto her tape. "When can I see you?" A jealous lover's message.

"Your machine didn't pick up right away, and I wondered if you had simply vanished without telling me. I tried to imagine how I would feel, but I couldn't, really." Dr. Marks smiled, amused by my bravado.

"Before we begin," she said, "I need to tell you that the Institute is raising its fees."

"Fine," I said in a silent fury. She always does this to me, I thought, waits for the moment when I am bursting with news and brings me back to the inescapable fact of our relationship — that this is therapy, that she is here because I pay her to be here.

So much for coming three times a week, I said to myself. I knew the subject would come up again soon — we'd been skirting it all spring — and now I had an easy excuse: with the fee hike I simply couldn't afford it. Therapy was beginning to resemble an old Victorian house whose restoration exceeds all budgetary estimations; unchecked, there seemed no limit to how much money such a project could consume.

"So," said Dr. Marks. "How was your summer?"

I shrugged. "It was OK, I guess. Not bad, not great." Ben was stuck, seemingly forever, in the terrible twos, and showed no interest in toilet training. David's new job precluded his staying up in the country with us — he joined us on weekends, as his own father had when he was young — but the commuting bothered me less than his impetuous decision to join a softball league that played on Sundays. Our truncated weekend thus began with his arrival late Friday night and ended a scant thirty-six hours later with his departure. As the season wore on we both became less adept at concealing our feelings; in fact, my resentment flared up in direct proportion to his glee.

One weekend my parents visited. Come Sunday morning, after David left for his game, my father found me in tears. He put his arm around me as if to say that David's desertion hurt and pained him too; David was acting childish, selfish. But I shrugged him off. I couldn't accept his compassion. How dare he judge my husband; he didn't understand. David found softball rejuvenating. My father would benefit from some of David's self-absorption, from David's ability to identify and secure what he needed. My father was altogether too selfless.

"So there I was, furious at everyone."

"Well, no one was giving you what you wanted. David wouldn't give up his softball game, Ben wouldn't give up his diapers, your father wouldn't give up his martyrdom."

"But how could I be angry at him? He was trying to help me. He was sympathizing with me. He was mad at David only because I was. The times I'm meanest to my parents are when I most resemble them. I'm condemning them for what I'm not."

"You aren't always reasonable," Dr. Marks said, but her voice held no reproach.

Yet even more unreasonable was my behavior during a

friend's week-long visit. One of her sons was roughly Ben's age, calm, collected, and toilet trained. Late one night the sounds of seven sleeping people woke me. I hate them, I said to myself; I hate them all for being asleep during my insomnia, I hate my friend's son for being toilet trained, my son for not being toilet trained, my friend's husband for loving my friend instead of me, my husband for loving me when I can be so horrible, so petty, so unbearable.

"That voice," I confessed, "I don't know where it comes from, but it's horrible. It speaks to me as if I were the worst person on earth, the blackest, vilest person."

"As if you didn't know the difference between feeling and acting," Dr. Marks continued. When I looked confused she said to me, "You don't have to act on all your feelings, do you?"

"It doesn't matter if I don't act on them. You know those signs, Don't Even Think of Parking Here? That's how I feel, as if I shouldn't even think these thoughts."

"Why not?"

"They're poisonous."

"What will happen?"

I couldn't answer.

"What will happen?" She was pushing me.

"Someone will die, I'll explode —" as soon as I said this aloud I could hear the absurdity of it.

"Your feelings will be responsible for the death of another human being, of an entire family . . ."

Now I was laughing; we both were, as the image of my friend going about her own life, unaware of and unharmed by my feelings, rose before me.

"It's crazy, I know," I said. "It reminds me of what happened last spring, when I didn't bring you flowers because I was angry at you for leaving me even though I was the one who was leaving you. It just doesn't make sense."

"Do feelings have to make sense?" Dr. Marks asked quietly.

She'd given me this kind of reply many times, but my attempts at understanding had pooled like water unable to seep through nonporous rock. This time her question penetrated as if there were a plumb line from my head to my heart. My feelings didn't have to be rational or reasonable, didn't have to be explained or apologized for, didn't have to be tamed or ignored; I could have them, hold them, even talk about them without damage to me or anyone else.

Something is happening, I said to myself suspiciously; something is different. Although Dr. Marks and I were sitting as we had sat a hundred times, speaking as we had always spoken, an unrecognizable element had injected itself into our meeting. That she was contributing more than ever, answering questions more directly, posing questions more pointedly, was only part of the change.

One of David's graduate psychology professors stands at the entrance to my high school auditorium, feeling the heads of the students filing in to see if anyone is feverish. The students in front of me are accepted, but I am stopped. The professor/doctor takes me aside and sadistically palpates my swollen glands until I wince in pain. David comes for me and asks the doctor what to do. "The best thing is to take her home, away from others, and have no money," the doctor says. Then he gives me an appointment for a year from now — "30 May 1985" — when I must report to the ear, nose, and throat clinic to be reexamined; the prescription is written on a piece of paper with a tiny piece of flesh taped to the bottom. David confers with the doctor. They talk for a long time. I hear less and less, I can't talk, I'm suddenly feeling worse, as if my throat were closing, I'm trying to get their attention but I feel fainter by the moment. I don't panic — I think, This is really it, I am feeling sicker, really sick, now they will take care of me, complete care, I am excused, it's indisputable, they are good men tending to me, taking me seriously.

"And what do you think this is about?" Dr. Marks asked.

I'd assumed that the dream was directly related to the partial mastectomy my mother had had to undergo a few weeks before. Dr. Marks asked what other associations I had with the dream.

I told her that the part about feeling faint and unable to talk paralleled an allergic reaction I'd actually had to some codeine that had been prescribed for a muscle spasm. "Anything else?" Dr. Marks asked.

"I wonder why the doctor told David we had to have no money?"

"It would make sense if the dream were about therapy," Dr. Marks said.

"I knew you were going to say that; you've said it about so many of my recent dreams, but I don't really understand why."

"There is a psychologist in it," she said, "and we've been talking for a while now about your fears that more therapy would deplete you financially."

"Meaning what?" I asked testily. "That's not a real fear?" I was trembling. My life was beginning to feel overrun by therapy; every time I looked up I was entering or leaving Dr. Marks's office. Yet in a paradoxical way, beginning my third year in therapy, I felt that I needed it less than ever. My day-to-day life was progressing smoothly enough: David was enjoying his internship, my mother's postsurgical prognosis was promising, my classes were going well. Only two recurrent topics irritated me — my coming to therapy three times a week, and Ben's refusal to be trained. That he wore diapers upset me terribly. He was getting closer to achieving control, but an invisible hurdle always seemed to finally defeat him.

I am in the kitchen of the apartment in which I grew up; it is spotlessly clean with no evidence of food. I am standing at the sink, and Gene, an old friend, is next to me. I'm drinking the most delicious coffee I've ever tasted, dark and sweet, from a crystal espresso cup, which keeps being refilled; I can drink as much as I like and there's always more. I don't have to share it. Gene knows how I am feeling and doesn't want me to stop or offer him any; he is happy just seeing how happy I am. I can take as much as I need.

"It sounds like a dream about nursing," Dr. Marks said.

"But with black milk."

"Well, it's a dream about contrasts," she offered. "I'm thinking of the spotless, sterile kitchen and the sense of overflowing supply, of someone who is waiting to be offered some but you don't have to share, someone whose happiness is your own."

I was weeping, the dream washing over me, filling me with longing. Imagine, the possibility of a limitless supply, of never having to worry about depletion or about exhausting the source of my sustenance. "I drank as much as I wanted," I cried.

"You still can," Dr. Marks said.

One morning at eight I received a phone call from a man saying he was Dr. Marks's husband: she was ill, he said, and wouldn't be able to keep our appointment later that day but would make up the session with me the following week.

"How did you feel when I had to cancel?" Dr. Marks asked when I saw her next. She sounded hoarse and looked pale.

"How could I feel? You were sick," I said, as if that were an answer. But before our next session I had this dream:

Ben stands alone in the lobby of our apartment building near the mailboxes, wearing a dirty diaper. I start to change him, but I have only shreds of tissues; shit begins oozing out of his diaper into my pocketbook, onto my clothes — everywhere. David finally comes down the stairs. "Where have you been?" I cry, furious that he has taken so long, that he has left Ben alone in such a state.

"So you were angry that we had to miss a session," Dr. Marks said.

"Maybe, a little," I stammered. I had to say it, had to admit to feeling a barely perceptible pressure on the paper-thin wall of a tiny interior room buried deep inside me, which I'd overlooked for many years. Yes I was angry, unreasonably angry; no, Dr. Marks didn't hate me for it. To absorb these statements seemed to require such enormous feats of concentration that I sat without moving and recited them over and over, as I had multiplication tables, until I felt sleepy — exhausted, really — anxious for therapy to be over so I could give my overworked brain a much-deserved rest.

But there was no rest, for in two days it was time for my next session, the third that week. I felt vertiginous, battered, almost abused by the prospect of yet another forty-five minutes: therapy was threatening to obliterate the rest of my life.

I am in Dr. Marks's office, a big room with just a couch along one wall. She is sitting in a chair across from me, wearing a purple silk blouse I have admired. I begin talking but suddenly she rises and sits down next to me and I lean over and she hugs me, caresses me. I touch her face — the perfect moment, just what I have always wanted. Then she announces that my therapy is done, I'm finished, and gets up to water her plants. Her office is suddenly swarming with plants. I start to cry, and she says not to worry, that she can see me as a friend next week at her home, though this office is really her home. As I walk toward her I knock over a watering can and water runs everywhere. Anxious, I check to see if she's angry or disgusted.

"I was angry at you in the end," I said, "because you left me for your plants, your other clients, and because you told me when I first began that I'd be the one who'd stop therapy, and in the dream you did. Even though you also offered me what I always want from you — your friendship. Except that in the moment you offered it I saw it wasn't what I wanted."

"Maybe you couldn't believe me, believe that I was telling the truth when I said you were finished."

Yes, that sounded right. I never trusted what I received, convinced that any rewards were ill-gotten, all the while valuing what I denied myself and craving what I didn't have. As much as I longed for Dr. Marks's embrace I knew I'd despise her if she ever offered it, a sure sign that she had allowed herself to be seduced by me.

"It's almost as if you were testing me in the dream," Dr.

Marks mused, "to see how messy you could be before I'd reject you."

"But there's always more messiness," I cried. "I feel so clumsy these days, clutzy, losing things, dropping things around the house." The night before I had shattered a glass pitcher we had received as a wedding present, and the night before that two cups and saucers from our stoneware. Later, reading in bed, I found myself in a reverie, wondering what it would feel like to have glass in my vagina. I told Dr. Marks this; suddenly I seemed powerless to withhold anything from her. "Maybe it's the sting of holding in your pee," she said.

"Shit and pee, pee and shit, that's all I think about, dream about; I can't stand it. I'm turning into a fucking toddler. I'm worse than Ben." Ben, for whose sake I was in therapy; Ben, the subject of my therapy, the subject through which I also studied myself.

"It takes a lot of energy to be neat," Dr. Marks said. I nodded as if I knew this, but I didn't. And then I remembered a moment in ninth grade biology when, beneath a more powerful lens, the seemingly inert drop of pond water we were microscopically examining suddenly, sickeningly, swarmed with life; thousands of tiny, swirling organisms, algae and paramecia, swam into view, and my stomach lurched — then and now. There seemed no end to the phenomena of which I had been unaware.

"I just feel different, out of control, so jumpy, at home in my life, and here too. It's as if I can't hold anything back, I have to say whatever I'm thinking, I don't process my thoughts as much as I once did."

"I see a difference too," Dr. Marks said.

"What do you mean?" I felt panicky, my breath quick.

"You seem freer here, as if you're relying less and less on a script, as if you've eased up about saying what's on your mind. Less worried about what I may think. Less concerned with controlling the flow of the sessions. I wonder if relinquishing some control here will enable you to take more control of your life."

"You mean, and come three times a week —"

"Maybe," she said. "If that's what you want. I think maybe you're ready to give yourself what you want. It's connected with that dream you had, the one in which you got sick and allowed that man to take care of you."

"It was as if I finally had confirmation, or permission to fall apart, to be sick —"

"To get help," Dr. Marks quickly cut in. "To loosen your grip on everything you had to keep so tight inside you."

I stumbled out of therapy that night in terror. How desperately I had longed for such a session, one in which Dr. Marks not only read my mind but offered to take care of me. Yet all I could think of was the boy who'd asked me to my senior prom. I'd pined after him, too, only to feel repulsed by him the moment he'd made his intentions known. That he liked me — that he was in my power — sickened me. Love me, love me, love me, I cried, but only until the moment that someone said I do. Then I had to flee. Since I couldn't imagine deserving love — only purchasing it — how could I love or respect someone who loved or respected me?

But how had I tricked Dr. Marks into giving me what I wanted?

I sat through my next appointment as if I were wearing a raincoat, hat, and galoshes — without getting my feet wet. I squandered the session, and every session for the next four weeks, by talking about the weather, my classes, my brother, petty arguments with David. As I chattered I watched her face to see if I felt repulsed by her or if she felt repulsed by me.

She never flinched, never wavered, acted as she had always acted. Finally I began to wonder if anything had happened. Maybe I was imagining a breakthrough where there had been none.

"I don't know what to call you," I began one evening in early January. "On your answering machine you say, 'This is Dr. Marks,' but when you leave a message on my machine you say,

'This is Alice Marks.' All my other friends call their therapists by their first names."

"You can call me Alice, if you'd like," Dr. Marks said with unnerving equanimity.

"I don't know what I want," I said. "I'm feeling so confused. That session we had a month ago, when you echoed my feelings that I was behaving differently, it was so pivotal to me that I had to waste all this time trying to figure out if you'd take it back, if you'd meant it. But I have to trust that you meant it. I'm not less of a person because I need help. This isn't a power struggle; it isn't a case of if you win, I lose. I kept putting my coming three times a week in those terms. But that isn't right. Coming three times a week is something I can give myself, something you can help me give. It's all so different from what I thought it would be."

Dr. Marks nodded but said nothing. I went on. "When I first started seeing you I thought that I was a very trusting person. It took me two years to see I wasn't. That's a long time." I paused. "I suppose it's not really such a long time." Dr. Marks smiled. "So many of my breakthroughs come in dreams. I wish that I'd been able to talk about some of these issues face-to-face."

"Some people don't break through at all," she said.

"I understand," I said. After two years I'd finally worked my way back to the beginning of understanding.

"What are you thinking about now?" Dr. Marks asked.

"Baseball," I said. For many years before I attended my first game I'd been a fan, yet I sat through the early innings feeling as befuddled as a visitor from India. Not until late in the game did I realize what was troubling me — there were no announcers narrating and interpreting the action. All around me fans were screaming, vendors were hawking hot dogs and beer, yet to me the stadium was strangely silent. On the field the players executed the same plays I'd seen hundreds of times, but even the most ritualized elements of the game — the conference on the mound, the pitcher's warm-up tosses — looked completely foreign and were imbued with an air of uniqueness. This was a purer, more essential form of baseball, a game that had been distilled by my heightened senses.

"And that's how I feel now," I told Dr. Marks, "as if I'm doing something I've done hundreds of times yet something is completely different, as if I'm in a totally strange and new place."

"I think you are," she said.

II

"How are you? What's new?" Friends called, I met acquaintances on the street, colleagues dropped by my office to chat. Everything was new, but not in the way they meant it. So I said nothing, not knowing where or how to begin, wondering if they believed me, if they noticed that I was as preoccupied as a foreign correspondent, earplug concealed, receiving round-the-clock bulletins from a tiny, far-off country known only to me, in a private, untranslatable language.

I am sitting in a room, a small room in a white suite of rooms. Sunlight streams in the window and a breeze billows the curtains. I am wearing a gauzy dress and sandals. I sit on the couch and study the door, afraid that it is locked even though I can see that it is open, wide open.

"You're going to therapy three times a week?" a friend asked. I was at her house for dinner; as we sipped wine our husbands sliced the roast. "I can understand going once or twice a week but *three times.* You don't seem as if you would need that much. Don't you worry about running out of things to say?"

Therapy had become part of my landscape. I saw Dr. Marks two days in a row, had a day off, came once more, then marked time through the weekend until my next session. The January days were short, and whether my appointments were scheduled for late afternoon immediately after teaching or early evening just after dinner, I arrived and left in frozen darkness. But I seemed to exist in contradiction to my surroundings, just as runners undaunted by winter find themselves sweating through their protective gear though their feet are wet from snow. Pregnancy had also occasioned such a defiance: oblivious of the winter that year, warmed by the engine of the fetus, I had felt my outer world dissolve, evanesce, defer to my internal weather. In the snow-laced, muffled city, Dr. Marks's office was a point of warmth whose power source, I sometimes felt, was me — my limitless, bottomless, effortless, feverish churning.

"Going to therapy three times a week," said a friend who knew, "is much different from going twice because you can't pretend that you don't remember what you were talking about the last time you were there."

The semester was off to a strange start. In seven years of teaching writing to both undergraduates and adults, I'd had my share of favorite students and entertained several pleasant flirtations. But this spring, for the first time, I found myself derailed by two thrilling infatuations. One man, a returning student who postponed taking the required freshman composition course I taught until his senior year, was exactly as old as I was. He was an excellent writer, and his essays inspired me to respond with long, encouraging comments, which he then annotated and augmented — a lovers' correspondence couched in pedantry. We met circumspectly in class for a month or so until he proposed, in the midst of a conference in my office about an essay he'd written, that we finish up over a cup of coffee.

"I don't usually do things like this," I said nervously, as we settled into a filthy but relatively quiet corner of the otherwise raucous student cafeteria.

"You mean, ah, this cross-cultural thing, right?" Andrew was black, enormously tall — a basketball star — married and the father of one son exactly Ben's age, who sometimes accom-

panied him to class and sat at a desk calmly drawing. I nodded.

"Yeah, I know what you mean," he sighed. "I never did either."

The essay we were putatively discussing was about his ath-
letic career and the ways in which he felt exploited by the ma-
chinery of collegiate sports. But I was much more interested in
his thoughts on the competitive spirit. He tried to explain how
badly he wanted the ball in a clutch situation, how thoroughly
he knew that he alone could sink the winning shot. "Give the
ball to *me*," he mugged, as if he were in the middle of the court,
shoving his teammates out of his face, his fingers itchy for action. "You have to have that killer instinct."

"I've never felt that, not for one second of my life," I said and
laughed. Impending crises on the playing field, in the faculty
room — anywhere — found me cringing to the point of invisi-
bility.

"Oh yes you have." Sometimes we switched roles: now he
was the teacher, I the student. "It's in there. You just forgot
where."

Thursdays I had a two-hour break between classes. One late
afternoon I visited Denise in her new apartment across town,
the one she'd described as large enough to comfortably host our
mothers' group each week. But since her move three months
ago none of us had seen or heard from her.

I gasped when I stopped inside. It was the kind of apartment
featured in the architectural pages of Sunday magazines. Its sin-
uous walls, painted in Southwestern ochers and pinks, swerved
and veered through a kind of maze, creating nooks and coves
and meandering hallways, culminating in the triumph of the ca-
pacious living room, whose focal point was an enormous window.

Denise prepared tea in her rose-colored kitchen — rose walls,
sink, gleaming ceramic tile. In her cabinets were shelves that

pulled out, built-in wine racks, lazy Susans, recessed spice holders that spun around to reveal even deeper recesses. "Tom went to school with a decorator," she said, attempting to explain how all this had come to pass.

We sat on a kind of urban verandah, a partitioned part of the living room facing the picture window. Even twelve stories up, with Madison Avenue funneling its brilliant way downtown, the space managed to convey the feeling that we were on some kind of frontier, the only settlement for miles around.

"This is unbelievable," I stammered. "I can't believe you live here. It seems like paradise."

"Believe me, it isn't." And in a choked voice she began to tell me why she hadn't been in touch with any of us from group: she and her husband were in marriage counseling. She wanted another baby; he didn't. "How can we have such different feelings?" she cried. "We're so distant from each other."

"I don't know," I said quietly.

"You and David wouldn't find yourselves in this situation, right? You're so much on the same wavelength. I've always seen that in you two."

We were both uncomfortably silent. "So," she said, perking up, "tell me what's new with you."

"Well, I'm in therapy three times a week now," I began, knowing I couldn't say anything more about that. But I did have something else to tell her if only I could spit it out. A publisher was interested in a book I wanted to write about the experience of being pregnant with Ben.

I saw in her eyes the same look I felt in my own when she opened the door to her apartment. "That's wonderful," she exclaimed, pressing my hand. She knew how long I had been struggling with my writing, how I had been tentatively sending essays to editors at magazines and book companies, and had dreamt of this moment. And yet behind her words to me I heard her say to herself, Be happy for her, be happy.

"But," I hastily added, "it's all preliminary and meanwhile

I'm running around worried about Ben, worried about my classes, afraid I'm doing everything half-assed and nothing well."

"Don't," Denise said. "Don't make yourself miserable on my account. You're working, you're being a wonderful mother, you have a good marriage. I envy you."

"But I envy you," I said, as if only one of us were entitled to that feeling. "I mean, look at this apartment. I live in an anthill by comparison. And Tom is all established in his career, and you don't have to work —"

"But I want to work," she interrupted. "Part-time jobs for lawyers are nearly impossible to find. I haven't gotten one offer. I'm nowhere."

"This is hard for us," we agreed, almost in unison, admitting to our mutual shame our reciprocal envy. We spoke on the edge of our seats, hurrying over our words, trembling from the sheer relief that we weren't alone, that someone else felt as we did, admitting what we had so long kept locked inside, as if we were college freshmen who'd stayed up all night in the fetid, deserted lounge, smoking cigarettes and spilling our guts to each other while everyone else in the dorm slept. In this orgy of confession I began to describe the flirtations I had enjoyed during the semester, and she haltingly acknowledged that she and Tom had been having marital problems for years.

"Maybe you should think about therapy," I suggested as gently as I could, as I began gathering my things to leave. I'd never warmed to her husband; I knew I couldn't give her anything resembling advice on how to proceed in her marriage.

"I know," Denise said, walking me to the elevator, our arms around each other's waists. An elderly neighbor setting out with her three poodles for a twilight walk probably thought us tipsy. "But I really think I just needed someone to talk to. I haven't been in touch with anyone for months, and I missed you so. I'll think about what you said. But thanks for this afternoon. Maybe you can come again next week. If we can talk, that's all I really need."

At the bus stop, I glanced up and saw Denise standing on her balcony, waving, removed from the full-blown rush hour being enacted all around me. The peacefulness of her apartment was fading, and in its place my familiar anxieties arose: Had the babysitter shown up? Had David remembered to take out Ben's dinner before he left? Would Andrew insist that I go out to lunch with him, off-campus, or would he let the subject gracefully drop? Would Henry, the other student in my life that semester, show up late again? Would he show up at all?

My bus lumbered to its stop, tilting to one side: the doors could barely wheeze open, and passengers crammed the stairs. I hitched up my briefcase, cradling it in my arms as I would an infant, and began walking downtown.

I opened each writing class I taught with a ten minute free-writing exercise during which I urged my students to write whatever came into their heads, no matter how scrambled, without worrying about the rules of grammar. "You can write it in code," I said to their amusement, "but you have to keep writing. If you get stuck just write, 'I'm stuck, I'm stuck,' until you get unstuck." The exercise was especially instructive for new writers: it taught them to value process over product, that one can't write and edit simultaneously, that there is invariably something to say.

I always wrote along with my students. That night I filled page after page with a letter to Denise, a letter I knew I'd never send, in which I carried our confessional a few steps further. "You have no idea," I wrote, "how envious I really am. I can't read letters from my graduate school friends, all writers, without first skimming the letter to make sure they had no huge successes to report." Sick, I'm sick, I'm vile and base and worse than anyone could possibly imagine because I keep all this garbage wrapped up in such a neat little package.

Have you hurt your friends? I heard Dr. Marks ask me. Have you actively sabotaged their careers? She never blinked or blanched, her eyes never widened or tightened when I told her about my triumphs or my failures. I would never see her apartment or meet her for coffee; I'd never sit next to her, touching knees as I had with Denise; we'd never walk down the hall with our arms around each other but now I knew why: I needed Dr. Marks to remain divorced from me even as our intimacy deepened, to maintain some neutrality, her absence from my life making possible her most significant presence.

"Oh, Denise," I wrote, "there were so many things I couldn't tell you, even as we sat so close to each other we could smell each other's perfume and see each other's skin under our makeup. I can't be impartial about your husband, he's such a jerk, just as you can't hear me talk about my ambivalences." Our talk had been lovely, and while it may have been therapeutic, it certainly wasn't therapy.

I looked up; Henry, who didn't know how to make an inconspicuous entrance, had come into the room and taken a seat near the window. He worked with juvenile delinquents in Staten Island and wore to my class what he had probably worn to peace marches fifteen years ago — turtlenecked sweaters, flannel shirts, dungarees, and work boots. He wrote stories about a young boy whose back yard abutted a cemetery. When he spoke up in class, which he did often, he managed to convince me that he was talking to me alone.

"What am I doing?" I'd asked Dr. Marks just last week. "I'm obsessed with these men — not one, but two. What's happening to me?"

"You're fantasizing," she said in a tone that allowed me to draw only one conclusion — that it was natural, that everyone did it, that I had done it in the past without knowing what I was doing. It was like free-writing, moving beyond embarrassment and fear to a place where the process took over, where what you said was less important than the fact that you were talking, dreaming, fantasizing, and trusting ("Trust me," I'd implore my skeptical students to whom free-writing sounded like one more dumb game in a desperate teacher's arsenal), that out of the unpunctuated chaos something would emerge some glimmer of understanding, of acceptance, of acknowledgment, of awareness that perhaps the door wasn't locked. Perhaps it had been open all along, and all I had to do was lean against it, push it open, and slip through.

III

I CAME INTO THERAPY lacing my boxing gloves, ready to spar. David and I had been shopping around for a new car, I hastily explained to Dr. Marks; our ten-year-old, hundred-thousand-mile Duster was racking up repair jobs faster than we could pay for them. After a month of fastidious consumer legwork we'd settled on a used but relatively pristine Saab — a safe, dependable car. When I told my father about our decision I met with a barrage of gratuitous advice. "Not only doesn't he give me any credit, he infantilizes me," I cried. "He told us to check *Consumer Reports*, for God's sake, as if we wouldn't have thought of that, he told us to shop around, can you believe it, as if we'd fall for the first deal we found."

"What did you want him to say?" Dr. Marks asked, the same question she had asked scores of times before, the question whose answer always seemed so infuriatingly vague and elusive. But this time the answer came to me encapsulated in a balloon I had only to pluck out of the air in front of me.

"I wanted him to say, 'That sounds like a good choice; good work and good luck.' " I wanted him to give me his blessing, just as Dr. Marks had a few weeks before during my breakthrough. She hadn't inundated me with advice, hadn't appropriated my success and made it her own.

"If all you want is his confirmation, then he has nothing to offer you," she said.

"He has the knowledge that he brought me up to have good judgment."

"Apparently he's not done bringing you up," Dr. Marks said. Her bland remark enraged me: Was she taking his side? Was she trying to talk me out of my feelings?

Oh my God, I panicked, sputtering, gasping for breath as if I were allergic to my own anger, is this it? Is this the session during which I bottom out? Collapse on the floor in an incoherent, ranting puddle of emotion?

I am on a yellow school bus. I have to get to a hotel in the middle of the city but all the numbers and streets are confused. In one hotel I see Michael, my old boyfriend; he is waiting for me. I tell him I have to go to the bathroom, and rush past him. The bathroom shelves are filled with cosmetics, which I am tempted to steal; in another corner I spot a paper bag full of old baby toys — Ben's toys, some of which I made for him — all broken, smashed, defaced, begrimed. I am heartbroken. When I find Michael again I tell him, "I am not beholden to you no matter how kind you are to me."

"A very sad dream," I said to Dr. Marks, thinking of Michael: I'd always felt bound to him by a contract I hadn't remembered signing but which he could produce, at will, with my signature indisputably affixed.

"It seems to have consolidated many concerns you have these days," Dr. Marks noted.

"Almost like the quilt I made for Ben," I mused, each patchwork square representing a discrete anxiety: toilet training, Michael, kleptomania. Even the cosmetics reminded me of the small bag of toiletries tucked into my mother's hospital drawer. She was in the hospital again for another test, another in a series of minor surgical procedures.

"I made that quilt for Ben before he was born. And it was in the dream, all dirty and torn and ragged."

"Is that what made you sad?" Dr. Marks asked.

"It was the first quilt I actually completed," I said. "I think babies should have things made by hand."

"But they shouldn't actually handle the handmade things."

"I let him use it. But not that much, I guess. He received so many other blankets when he was born."

"So you made it mostly for show."

"I just wanted it to last until Ben was old enough to understand, to appreciate it, to know that I had made it for him with my own hands, out of love." But I was defensive now. Of course I saw her point. In my family we bestowed our feelings upon special objects and imbued these icons with the burden of permanence while the feelings themselves — so impractically fragile, delicate, vulnerable to destruction — were tucked away in an emotional bank vault for safekeeping. We valued feelings in the abstract, greeting them as we would distant cousins with whom we are feuding, offering only a stiff, formal handshake when forced to meet at a party, belying any deeper connection.

Yet the very genes causing this affliction, which I'd inherited from my parents as they had from theirs, had mutated when passed on to my son. Ben forced me every day to remove the plastic slipcovers in which I'd ensheathed my feelings, to get down on the floor and tussle with them. Despite all my anxious injunctions about wear and tear he went blithely about his business, treating toys as if they were meant to be played with rather than shellacked into permanence, as if colorful patchwork quilts were made to be slept under, tangled up, used as picnic tablecloths, Superman capes, or space stations, and not hung on the wall like some museum piece, a testament to a mother's devotion. What he loved best he used most incautiously: he was eviscerating his beloved panda, Minnie, burrowing a hole in her back and removing all the stuffing, literally loving her to death. And while I was unquestionably grateful for his glorious immunity, it nonetheless reminded me of the embeddedness of my own condition. Don't tear it, don't break it, I'd involuntarily whisper, tiptoeing through his rough-and-tumble room, wincing each time he reached for something, skewered between my parents' diffidence and my son's temerity.

"Every psychological change involves some kind of violence." The line had jumped out at me from one of David's textbooks, and now I recited it to Dr. Marks.

"What's the violent change you're feeling?" she asked.

"I'm not sure." But the quilt was still on my mind. And so were the night-light wars.

Ben had always been a remarkably good and sound sleeper. Just recently he had noticed the darkness, as if for the first time. In the five-and-ten I bought a brown night-light with a detachable, swiveling shade; plugged in, it looked like an insect unfortunate enough to have gotten itself impaled in an electrical outlet. Worse, Ben insisted that the light was too dim. He wanted the overhead light switched on. All right, I agreed, thinking that once he fell asleep I could go in and switch it off.

The moment I did he'd jolt awake, as if I'd tripped an alarm rigged to his pillow. "On!" he'd order. I'd obey, tiptoe back to bed, and return a few minutes later when I was sure he'd drifted back to sleep. Like a tiny sentinel he'd be standing at his post, his hand cupped over the switch. "On!" he'd shriek. "Off," I'd insist.

And there I'd stand, at three in the morning, engaged in precisely the kind of battle of wills parents are not supposed to allow themselves to be maneuvered into, one from which there was no negotiable, satisfactory way out.

"Did you need a night-light?" Dr. Marks asked.

I remembered needing to stay up until my parents returned from their very occasional night out, but otherwise liking the dark. I liked waking up in the middle of the night, fishing for my slippers and bathrobe, and groping my way down the hall to the bathroom with eyes closed as if I were blind.

"What is it about the darkness?" she asked.

"I just like it," I said. I still liked to get out of bed for a drink, peer out the windows to see who among my faceless neighbors was also awake, and end up in what was the geographical center of our apartment, the spot from which I could glance into every room, study my husband and son bound up in sleep, and prayerfully repeat to myself, No one needs me now. Everyone who needs me is sleeping. No one will need me again for hours. "It's as if I'm inaccessible," I said.

"Invisible," Dr. Marks mused.

"It's the only time I can have to myself without denying myself to someone else."

"Who else are you beholden to?" Dr. Marks asked gently.

I shrugged. What was she driving at?

"I'm thinking of that dream about Ben's toys in the hotel, and about your recurring nightmare." She meant the one in which I return home and find that David has left and Michael is my husband, and he is so kind and grateful and gentle to me, but I know that it is all a terrible mistake — he's the wrong man and there won't be an end to how wrong he is — that my last chance for happiness is gone forever.

"How did you end the relationship with Michael?" Dr. Marks asked.

"I called him, long distance, and told him that I wasn't moving to Colorado to be with him. That I was staying in New York with David. But the only reason I did it was because David finally lost patience with me. I'd taken him to a friend's wedding, and was miserable during the ceremony. How come everyone else was entitled to happiness and not me? I had too much to drink, and during a dance with David I said, 'You don't like me when I drink, do you?' And he got furious at me — it must have been building up for that whole year — and said I was the one doing the rejecting, not him. So the next day I called Michael. We were on the phone for three hours, both of us in tears. 'Don't do this to me,' he kept crying. David waited upstairs at a friend's apartment. When it was all over, at about three in the morning, he came downstairs and we fell asleep in our clothes." Remembering the drama of that night, of my friend's wedding, of that entire year, of the dream that still visited me, even after seven years of marriage, I was crying again.

"You're more comfortable being rejected than rejecting," Dr. Marks said. "You're afraid to say no."

"But I'm also afraid to say yes."

"Maybe you have trouble saying yes because at some point you worry that you'll have to say no."

"I seem to sign on with people, create a kind of pact that says what's good for the other person is good for me too. But I feel pressured into signing, and then powerless to say no. And that's what was so frustrating about our relationship at first," I said to Dr. Marks. "You didn't offer me anything in return. You wouldn't let me relinquish myself in exchange for —"

"In exchange for what?" she interrupted, as if this were important.

"For care, for comfort, I guess, for protection, for love." I paused, trying to understand as I was speaking. "I give up myself and receive love. Then the other person has the power. Or at least he makes me think he has the power. Maybe I still do."

"No wonder you're confused. The boundary between selfishness and selflessness begins to blur in the kind of pact you describe. And don't forget, someone who's powerless wields an awful lot of power. What's good for him isn't always and necessarily good for you."

"David wants us to have another baby," I said, surprising even myself. I'd been meaning to talk about this with Dr. Marks, and had inadvertently deferred it, only to have it ambush me now.

"And you?" she asked. I explained that although we both had agreed that we wanted another child, we hadn't begun to talk about timetables. Then the week before, when we'd slept over at my parents' house, as Ben watched "Sesame Street" and my father prepared breakfast and my mother slept, David mumbled, "Don't bother with that," when I reached for my diaphragm. Caught off guard, I didn't protest.

After making love David had dozed off, but I was cursedly awake, staring into the corners of my old bedroom. Was I ready for a baby? Was Ben? I remembered him as he'd watched dry-eyed when his crib was disassembled and carted out to make way for his new big-boy bed, a present for his third birthday. "No diapers tonight," he'd announced, and sure enough he stayed dry while I worried the night away, awake and running to the bathroom every ten minutes, checking on my son who had just declared his own transition out of babyhood. Maybe David was right to think about a new baby.

"But you're not sure," said Dr. Marks.

"I'm not sure another baby is what I want, and I'm not sure this is the right time." I felt myself approaching a sealed door, a door I didn't want to open, but Dr. Marks pressed on.

"What happens if you say no?" Dr. Marks asked.

No. Ben could inflect this mite of a word a thousand different ways — he could savor it, spit it, protract it, hand-deliver it; the word *no* was his calling card, his ticket to autonomy, his proclamation of "I'm not you." Slowly there appeared before me a mournful parade headed by my father, Michael, my brother, men I went out with, men imploring me to go out with them, to sleep with them, to give up my plans and endorse theirs. Women appeared too, asking for friendship, for anything I didn't feel at the moment like supplying: I relived each juncture at which a single tiny word would have rescued me. "Don't leave me, don't reject me," these importunate shadows called, and time after time I had swallowed my resistance and was left gagging.

"I'll be left behind, somehow," I offered tentatively.

"Maybe you're the one who's leaving, and you're the one

who's angry," she said. "And that's too uncomfortable for you. You're more comfortable seeing yourself as victimized than as angry."

"But what's the point?" I exploded. "Nothing happens because you get angry, nothing good."

"You came in here pretty angry," Dr. Marks reminded me. "You were pretty angry at your father."

"But not angry enough, apparently. If I had really let out my feelings then I wouldn't be sitting here recounting how I felt."

"In other words," Dr. Marks interjected, "if you survive your anger you didn't get angry enough. The only real anger is that which annihilates both you and the object of your anger."

"Something like that," I said meekly, for I couldn't deny how strongly I had felt when I began. Yet here I sat, forty-five minutes later, still intact, while thirty miles away my father went about his business, unscathed by my outburst. "I'm not beholden to you," I'd said in the dream.

"How do you feel now?" Dr. Marks asked.

I took a deep breath. Let's see. I felt tired, sad — not depressed, but saddened. Like a hapless border state whose sovereignty was constantly disputed, I felt the accumulated weight of too many years of revolving allegiance settle onto my shoulders with almost palpable force. I wanted to exist unto myself, a nation within me, borders shored up, secure and unshifting.

I did, of course, exist that way. I knew it. My father knew it. We were separate people no matter how much noise he made to the contrary. We could love each other even if our needs didn't always dovetail. I knew how to say no.

I felt as if I'd been up for days. "Maybe I've actually taken a small step forward," I said tentatively.

"Not so small," she said.

"Why do I force you to tell me that?" I said. "Why can't I reassure myself?"

She smiled. "I don't mind," she said.

IV

"SOME TIME in the next month or so," Dr. Marks began one afternoon in April, "I may have to take some time off. But I'll let you know."

Great, I thought. There I was, feeling swamped, powered by a manic energy that always took over when I was feeling most stressed, only to have Dr. Marks, my one constant, my polestar, allude to life's inherent unpredictability. Not too long ago I would have pondered her declaration as if I were an intelligence officer stubbornly poring over a particularly recalcitrant scrap of information: What did she mean, some time off? How long? Why didn't she know when? But I was past pondering her situation and through with wishing we could meet in her apartment for coffee. I needed her right there in that chair, feet up, in her familiar dresses and shoes, her hair just so, looking directly at me, helping me cope with a thicket of threatening crises: David and I were trying to conceive and not succeeding; he was changing jobs; Ben, though urine-trained, still wanted diapers for bowel movements; I still nursed my infatuations; my mother was in the hospital again after a mammogram revealed a tumor in her other breast; and just last night I'd found out that a friend from graduate school who'd been overseas for two years was stopping by for an overnight visit with her boyfriend, whom I'd never met.

"Sounds like you need another pair of hands," Dr. Marks said, as I sat ticking off my troubles one by one.

I wasn't in a joking mood. Our tiny room and our circumscribed conversation had generated an enormous mansion of discourse, and my entire world seemed infected by therapy, not in the sense that anyone else was therapeutic, but that every encounter or exchange took on a therapeutic cast. I couldn't separate or tease out my actual life from dreams or therapy; the categories of my experience had bled into each other. What would begin as a normal, innocuous conversation with my mother, my department chairman, my super, or an acquaintance would take a strange turn, and I'd hear myself as if I had suddenly put my fingers in my ears or was speaking in the shower, my words amplified, reverberating, full of significance, heavy as stones.

"How do you feel about seeing your friend?"

Excited. Nervous about meeting her boyfriend. Wishing just she and I could rent a hotel room and spend time together. But who had time to dwell on feelings when I was drowning in logistics: Where would they sleep? Our apartment was so tiny. How would we all eat? Our kitchen table sat only three. What kind of food did they like? Yesterday I'd torn through the shelf that served as a linen closet, tossing out the pilly sheets, the ratty towels, looking for a presentable set. I'd never have time to clean the kitchen. The furniture hadn't been vacuumed in months.

Only two weeks ago I'd felt so calm. I remembered a Sunday morning that found Ben watching television in the living room and David dozing. At the kitchen table in my bathrobe, ignoring last night's unwashed pots and dirty dishes, I transcribed the dream I'd just had into my journal: *The editor who is interested in my pregnancy book comes to my house to talk with me about an idea I proposed for an article — about bad friends. Though she had initially rejected the proposal she is now thoroughly enthusiastic, and as her con-*

*versation becomes increasingly animated I rifle through my desk drawers
to find the manuscript. "Never mind that, dear," she says, beginning to
dictate page after page of wonderful material, and all I have to do is
copy it down and it becomes my novel, my long-dreamed-of novel.*

Quite spontaneously at the kitchen table, I switched into free-
writing and began an article about finding private time for work
even in the midst of chaos. I couldn't write fast enough. Form
and content came together, the feverish pace of my writing prov-
ing the very point I was striving to make — that if I didn't have
to wrest this small chunk of time from the insatiable maw of
family life, that if I had had an entire morning in front of me
rather than the probable ten minutes until Ben asked for a glass
of milk and more cereal, I'd still be in bed. I should be cleaning
up, getting dressed, playing with Ben, cooking breakfast, buying the paper, returning phone calls: this litany ran through my
head like a ticker tape, but from some hidden recess within me
I was able to push aside all the "shoulds," ignore them, over-
power them, as if they offered no more resistance than the dirty
silverware. This was what I felt like doing now; even if the article I was working on never was published, I had all the reason
I needed to continue: *at this moment I feel like writing.*

But that morning seemed years ago. Whatever had fueled my
self-possession, my confidence, my impetuousness, had long
since burned itself out.

*An autopsy is performed on my cousin Lily's body. Traces of heroin and
other drugs are found in her blood.*

"It's the anniversary of Lily's death," I told Dr. Marks. "I suppose that's why I had the dream. Lily was a very good person,"
I continued, "everyone liked her. Even people who didn't get
along with anyone else liked her. She was very self-sacrificing."

Dr. Marks sat silent as I squirmed in my seat.

"I can't believe I'm envious of a dead woman," I finally
blurted out.

"You just want to be liked," Dr. Marks said.

"But you can't give and give without paying any attention to yourself. I can't always think about everyone else. But I suppose I wish I could."

"You feel as if you have to offer something to someone in exchange for his or her affection and love."

"How else does someone like you?"

"Just for being yourself, perhaps."

"But I'm not that good," I said.

"Maybe that wasn't Lily in the dream," Dr. Marks suggested. "Maybe that was you. Maybe you feel as if you have to deaden yourself, anaesthetize yourself, to get the ugly stuff out."

My parents had visited over the weekend, I told Dr. Marks. My father had asked if I had any silver polish, and when I opened the cabinet beneath the sink, bottles and jars spilled out onto the floor. "If you put things away neatly you'd find them more easily," my father had admonished.

Maybe those were the chemicals that turned up in Lily's body. My body. The thick, copper U-shaped pipe below the sink a kind of artery. "In the past three weeks," I told Dr. Marks, "I've shed three friends."

"An interesting verb," Dr. Marks said, but accurate. I had shed them as a dog sheds an old coat or a snake old skin; in many ways they had clung to my body by their fists the way baby monkeys grab their mother's hair, and I wanted to shake or shiver them off. In the guise of friendship they'd preyed on me, provoked me, undermined and hurt me.

"Lily had lots of friends like that," I said. "She'd still have them."

"And you don't," Dr. Marks said. "Maybe you don't need them anymore. That's why animals molt; the lost hair is useless."

What did it mean, not to need them? What if they were walking around, talking to mutual friends, to strangers, about what an awful person I was? How could I defend myself? "I wanted to tell my father to mind his own business, how I organized my sink was my business. But how could I, with all the bottles and jars in a heap around me? He was right. I was always such a neat person. But what if I'm really not?"

"What if," she said, not really a question.

"Under my sink —" I began, and Dr. Marks cut me off: "You seem to be spending a lot of time down there."

"Not enough, apparently," I said. "When I started to clean things out I found an infestation of some kind of insect, tiny little maggots flying around, nesting under a rag; I spent hours cleaning it all out, it was the most disgusting thing I've ever done."

"You're cleaning a lot these days," Dr. Marks said. I reminded her that Monica and her boyfriend were arriving over the weekend.

"Well, the first thing they'll probably do is check to see if the oven is scoured, the freezer defrosted, and the sink cabinet organized," said Dr. Marks, and I was suddenly furious at her, hating her sarcasm, never having heard it before.

"I can't help myself," I cried. "I care what they think of me."

"Do you really think they care what your freezer looks like?"

"I care."

"Do you?"

Did I? Did I care about cleanliness intrinsically or was it an offering I made to people, as if to say, I can clean up after myself? Or was it simply another arena in which I could show how I excelled? I was astonishingly fastidious; the only criteria I didn't meet were my own and my parents', for whom cleanliness was godliness. Scrubbing my way toward sainthood, I never realized as clearly as I did right then that I'd never achieve my goal in their eyes, and that no one else cared. *No one else cared*, except those whose minds would not be changed. I was squandering my energy, my time, my talent, in an unwinnable war, approaching the open door and bolting it shut instead of slipping through.

I've just come from the supermarket and I ask a burly man to help me move bags of groceries from car to house. He makes the first trip; when I enter my kitchen I see two mounds of oozing refuse. "Help me," I cry; why isn't the man here helping me? But he is in the bedroom tending the baby, and the groceries are still not unpacked. Suddenly I hear my mother's footsteps; she's about to come into the kitchen.

"It was my worst nightmare since childhood," I gasped to Dr. Marks. How did I manage to get through the time between my dream and this session? I'd sat up in bed as if electrocuted, waking David, nearly waking Monica and her boyfriend, who slept on the other side of the curtained French doors; I was trembling, crying, shaking, scared, out of breath.

"It was like a suppurating, unstaunchable wound, the flow of garbage," I cried. "How can I live like that, how did it get there, how could I have kept it a secret, what can I do?"

"Do?" Dr. Marks asked once and I gave in to tears. I couldn't seem to stop them. The vision in the dream, betraying my self-disgust, my infantile fears, was one I wished I'd never had. "Don't say that," I used to plead with David in the midst of a terrible fight, as if his angry words could sear my flesh or indelibly brand me. But though I'd forgotten all his words, I knew with dread certainty that this dream would sit in the bottom of my stomach, undigested, forever.

I am sitting in a small auditorium with Dr. Marks, watching a play. Monica joins us, and she and Dr. Marks walk off together. I stand up and yell "I'm gypped!" at the top of my lungs. When the curtain falls I see a brilliant red stain on it, a stain of menstrual blood.

"A spot of red; it reminded me of the Japanese flag," I volunteered.

"Hiroshima," she said.

"That's ridiculous," I said.

"What is?"

"Your likening my period to Hiroshima."

"You're trying to get pregnant," she said.

I was furious with her, sick to death of her and her glib, instant analyses. How could it possibly be? I thought to myself throughout that session and on the bus uptown and in bed that night while sleep eluded me. I drank some tea; I walked through the apartment, I rocked in the rocking chair where I had nursed Ben and slowly, as my body relaxed, I allowed myself to think for just a fraction of a moment that it could be — in fact it was true — that I greeted each period with a sickening fury as if it were a personal holocaust. My rage at my body, at David, at nature, was obscene. I wasn't even sure I wanted this baby, *and now I couldn't have one?* I wanted to flush myself, to erase myself; I was unspeakably sick of myself and my unending neediness, my limitless inadequacies, and everything I couldn't have.

When I woke up the next day I felt mysteriously cleansed. For the first time in weeks I could write in my journal. Walking Ben to day care and taking the bus to class, I found myself singing. That evening, Dr. Marks phoned and said she wouldn't be able to make our appointment that night or any next week. We'd meet again after that as usual. Fine, I thought, and I set about making a cake that David and I could share after Ben was asleep.

At our next appointment I told Dr. Marks that I had a good story for her. It was income tax time, and my parents, who prepared David's and my return, had noticed how much money David and I were paying for therapy. What concrete evidence did we have, they asked, that it was working?

" 'Concrete,' they said," I chortled to Dr. Marks, "as if we could come up with a shopping list of accomplishments." Dr.

Marks smiled. She looked a bit tired. "How was your vacation?" I asked.

"I wasn't really on vacation," she said, pausing. "Actually, my mother has been very sick, and last week she died."

She glanced down as she spoke. My heart pounded, my face flushed; I felt dizzy and faint and out of control. *Her* mother? I'd spent huge chunks of sessions for the past year talking about my mother's illness, and then her mother dies?

"I don't know what to say," I stumbled. "I feel terrible. I'm so sorry." Dr. Marks accepted my condolences wordlessly. How ridiculous of me to have even thought she had been on vacation. Looking at her now, seeing how haggard and drained she looked, I realized why she hadn't known when she would need to take off time from work. The puzzle pieces fit together now. But hadn't it been hard for her to listen to me as I ran on about my mother? How had she stood it? How could she stand it now?

"I didn't know. I should have been more sensitive."

"You can't blame yourself for not knowing," she said.

I did blame myself. I seemed to be experiencing every feeling I'd ever had at once; sitting across from my bereaved therapist was like looking into the mirror and seeing kaleidoscopic fragments of myself and everyone I'd ever cared about. She'd lost her mother, and my own mother was sick, and she was a kind of mother to me, and I was someone's mother, and the pain I felt was for all of us, all of us at once both lost and grieving, our nervous systems fused, or confused, as sometimes happens after making love, holding your lover and neither one can tell from the midst of the embrace whose heart is beating, who is coughing or laughing or breathing. I lost my voice as I had in those dreams, for words, even shouted words, couldn't be heard over the thunderous wave of emotion which snatched me up as all the feeling I had for Dr. Marks crested high above me and I closed my eyes, helpless in the inevitable undertow.

V

THE DOOR to Dr. Marks's suite was locked. Five minutes early for my appointment, I sat in a chair in the lobby with my sopping raincoat still buttoned, my briefcase in my lap. The doorman and elevator operator kept each other company, the lobby their private living quarters until a resident entered, occasioning a swift fade into obsequiousness. But I wasn't a resident — they knew which door I frequented — and they were unsure of how to treat me, what measure of distance or respect to accord me. I busied myself in the newspaper.

An umbrella whooshed closed, a woman shook the rain off her coat, removed her rain hat, fumbled for her keys in her pocket. Running late, Dr. Marks hurried to her door and let it slam shut behind her as if she hadn't seen me. Maybe she hadn't. Maybe the rain made me invisible, anonymous, a name in an appointment book.

I'd had a dream the night before. *It is raining on my way to therapy and I have to cross Central Park to get there. I try to take refuge under a bridge but some men find me and start to chase me. They have knives. They want to rape me.*

I didn't need Dr. Marks to help me figure it out. I was afraid of this morning's session, afraid that because of her own pain she wouldn't be able to shelter me. "Dr. Marks," I began, "I was going to write you a condolence card, because I'm good at those, but then I realized that would be silly. Why give you a card when I can tell you to your face, that I'm very, very sorry for your loss." Dr. Marks listened solemnly — she looked only slightly less haggard than last time — and said thank you.

"I want to ask you how you are" — the urge was so strong to stop these heartfelt, if prepared, remarks, and worry after her, act like a normal human being and ask after her grief as I would any other person, even a stranger — "but I'm afraid that I really don't want to know. I'm sure you have others to help see you through. If you came to work today I have to assume that you're ready to have a regular session."

She nodded. I'd said it: I didn't have to take care of her for her to take care of me; she didn't need me but I needed her. And this was all right. This was fine. This was what we had contracted for. I may not have expressed myself eloquently but I'd said something. I'd broken through my reluctance to speak unless my sentiments were perfectly phrased, and accepted that the offer of any words — even clumsy, awkward words — was infinitely more welcome than silence.

For the rest of the session I was visited by the eerie sensation that I'd become huge. I'd had this delusion before but only at night before sleep; this was its first daylight, public appearance. As long as I was looking at some part of my body I felt intact, but if I looked at Dr. Marks, or at her books, or at the water pooling around our umbrellas standing in the corner, my limbs swelled and I felt as if there were yards and yards of skin and sinew separating my hand from my elbow, my knee from my ankle. My proprioceptive sense was askew, and Dr. Marks, diminutive in her grief, seemed to shrink in direct proportion to my inflation, so that by the end of the session I worried about brushing against her, as if there were room in the modest office for only one of us and that person, it seemed, was me.

Dr. Marks and I are in a room with twin beds arranged exactly as my bedroom at my parents' house was arranged. We get into bed together.

There is a huge plate of food — cherries, pears, chocolate. We begin talk-
ing and eating, the food gets in the covers, I spill milk on the sheets. "I
want her to die," I say to Dr. Marks, about a woman we both know, and
we laugh ourselves silly. "I know what your dirty little secret is," Dr.
Marks says. "You want to have a rollicking good time, just like this."

Dr. Marks smiled when I told her this dream. But I was
confused: asleep I was free to spill milk on her sheets, yet
Ben's accidents, his failure to train himself, sent me into an uncontrollable towering fury, which found me slamming doors,
stamping my foot, imploding with foul language. Lest I turn my
son into someone who dreams of oozing garbage or weeps at
the sight of a messy kitchen sink cabinet I had been extremely
patient with him. Until now. He was almost three and a half.
Enough, I told myself, was enough.

One day, after yet another accident, I called Ben's pediatrician. He suggested that when Ben asked for a diaper in which
to move his bowels, I make him stay in the bathroom instead of
allowing him to run around as he wished. Ben didn't like this
new development; he cried and kicked for his freedom. But I
grounded him until he was done.

"That sounds very reasonable of you," Dr. Marks said.

"Really?" My antennae were up. For months she'd supported
me in my decision not to pressure Ben, to separate his needs for
control from mine. Yet now she sounded very pliant and ame-
nable, much like the pal I had once wished her to be, as if she
were dissolving the therapeutic gulf she'd once so systematically constructed. Whence this eagerness to second anything I
said? Why did she suddenly volunteer her reactions, even when
I hadn't asked her? Was she trying to get rid of me, now that I'd
had a big breakthrough? Was our real work over and this simply
the mop-up?

Of course, my big breakthrough had been about trust — spe-
cifically, trusting her — and here I was hobbled by suspicion.
How close to the end of therapy could I be?

"You always supported my decision not to rush him," I said, as if this would catch her in her own trap.

"But you're describing the situation differently now," she retorted. "You're not taking away his diapers; you're not saying to him, 'Now it's time to be an adult.' All you're saying is when you defecate you do so in the bathroom." I sat in silence. She made it sound as if it was within my rights to set a limit on some of his behavior.

Within the week, Ben was completely trained. "Now I worry that it happened too soon, before I could resolve *my* issues about toilet training," I moaned at my next appointment.

"You mean your feelings of helplessness, of powerlessness," Dr. Marks ventured.

"Well, take Monica's visit," I began. The visit had been troubling in many ways. Her boyfriend from England had a rhythm all his own — he slept late, stayed up late, and hogged the bathroom. But worst of all was that neither of them seemed to admire Ben to my satisfaction. "I know I want her to see him through my eyes and that's unreasonable of me —"

And then something almost miraculous happened. I interrupted myself to say, "No, it isn't. It isn't unreasonable." I could want anything at all — *anything*. My wanting didn't impinge on anyone else; all my desires were contained in me, no matter how outrageous, consuming, unreasonable. They exerted no implicit pressure, didn't blister or swell; they were private symptoms, not verifiable signs. *I could feel anything I wanted.*

"You know," I began, "we've started giving Ben M&M's when he doesn't use his hands to settle a dispute. Maybe I should reward myself with candy each time I'm true to myself."

"That's exactly the point," Dr. Marks said, "all your life you received goodies for suppressing yourself and now you have to learn a new way."

I felt like clapping my hands like a toddler who had to use her whole body to express delight. Oh, Dr. Marks, you put things so clearly, you clarify without simplifying, you allow me to digest these insights one kernel at a time. But time was up and I left without complimenting her wizardry. I had to trust that she sensed my gratitude.

"You won't believe what I did," I began one morning. Over the weekend Ben had proclaimed his graduation from bottle to cup. After our cheers died down, he asked what happened to the bottle now. Would it just sit there in the cabinet? Extemporizing, I explained that all the bottles big kids have outgrown go to Mr. Bottle, who recycles them by sending them to babies who need them. Together Ben and I affixed to the bottle a piece of masking tape, on which I wrote, "Mr. Bottle, Bottleland, USA," and on our morning walk he proudly tossed it into the mailbox. "Why am I telling you this?" I interrupted my chattering, suddenly doubly embarrassed that I'd done the stunt at all, and then that I'd confessed it to Dr. Marks.

"Maybe because you mailed away something of yours as well," Dr. Marks said, smiling.

"Something of mine?" I asked, screening the past weekend in my mind and freezing the action at the moment on the Long Island Expressway when, engrossed in conversation with David, I'd quite naturally and effortlessly downshifted in our new car; when, after two months of stalling at traffic lights and tollbooths, of swearing that buying this car with a manual transmission was the biggest mistake we'd ever made, I'd finally overcome my stiffening resistance, buried my fury, and let my body feel its way to coordination. In an instant, driving the car switched from an exercise in self-torture to a challenging pleasure.

"Of course, I began worrying that one day this car would break, and what if our next car wasn't a stick shift?" I said. "As soon as I start enjoying myself I worry that it's going to end. But it doesn't have to. We can buy other cars with stick shifts."

"Pleasure doesn't always have to be rationed out," Dr. Marks said.

Enough's enough; don't overdo it; you'll use it up: these were the maxims of my childhood, declaring that pleasure was powered by a battery whose charge inevitably petered out; that pleasure was not only as dangerous as radioactive uranium but quick to decay.

"Anything worth doing is worth doing well" was another of my father's favorite adages, one he recited with almost Scriptural reverence. I'd never thought to question it — until now. For months I'd been thinking of purchasing a computer and word-processing software to help me with my writing. I knew nothing about computers, and could do nothing, I assumed, until I was completely computer-literate.

But one afternoon, on impulse, I'd ventured into a computer store and begun to talk to a polite salesman. He didn't condescend to me or laugh at my tentative questions but instead persuaded me to sit down at a keyboard and peck out a few commands, which enabled me to formulate some more questions. I took notes, took home some literature, read it, and returned. I went to other stores. For weeks I deliberated, the computer a weight on my soul, a heaviness in my dreams. It was a huge financial undertaking, and I wasn't an expert. But maybe I didn't need to be. Maybe I didn't need to know everything about computer technology in order to buy a computer. Maybe it was better to do something pretty well than not do it at all.

"You're chipping away," Dr. Marks commented, bringing me close to tears. "Chipping" was right, as if I were attacking a formless chunk of marble with a sculpting tool the size and strength of a toothpick. Yet as much as I despaired of progress, when I looked down I saw dust and tiny pebbles at my feet, irrefutable evidence of work.

*

I am sitting on the floor in front of the kitchen sink, killing roaches that come out of the cabinet in waves. My father sits beside me; we are both crying, and he says, "It's OK, everyone has them, it's not your fault."

"The semester ended well," I said to Dr. Marks in the evening session following my last classes. Bidding good-bye to my two star pupils had turned my infatuations into nothing more than flirtations I had enjoyed but outgrown. Andrew, the athlete, had lingered after his afternoon final, urging me to meet him later for a drink; I agreed but in the end chickened out, leaving a note of regret taped to my office door along with his grade: an A, which, I assured him, he'd richly deserved. Henry, on the other hand, left the room not two minutes after I'd asked my students for an evaluation of the class. No sooner was he out the door than I pounced on the paper he'd deposited on my desk: "Never change," it read.

"What's ahead?" Dr. Marks asked. I admitted to her that for the first time in years David and I were delaying and abbreviating our annual Berkshires vacation. Because he was changing jobs and my mother was undergoing chemotherapy and I wanted to write, we decided to stay put in the city until mid-August, which also meant that I could continue therapy over the summer. Or I could end therapy as I always had at the end of June and bank the money I'd save. Hmm. From a great distance, as if I were separated by miles from her, I talked with perfect composure about the factors militating against continuing therapy — tradition, which left me on my own for the summer; my need to focus exclusively on my book; our precarious financial situation; my mother's impending treatment, all the phases of which I'd have to coordinate. Dr. Marks listened silently, nodding, caught up in my controlled detachment.

On my way out I stopped in the tiny bathroom to wash my face, only to find myself collapsing on the closed toilet seat, crying into my cupped hands, tears for my mother, for me, for

Dr. Marks too. How could cancer happen, how dare my mother get sick, how could this happen to me? I cried until I couldn't anymore. Then I got up and walked slowly to the bus stop. I stopped in a jewelry store and bought myself a pair of mother-of-pearl earrings without even inquiring first about the price. I bought flowers. As soon as I got home, I put on my favorite Billie Holiday record, and slipped into a hot bath. Then I put on perfume, draped a scarf over my blouse, and tried on my new earrings.

"What's the occasion?" David asked; I didn't usually dress up around the house.

"Just a whim," I said, stroking my new earrings, the pearl very pleasing to the touch, smooth and cool, unyielding even in its papery thinness. That night I had a dream: *At the end of a session Dr. Marks tells me what I have always wanted her to say: "You've worked so hard, it's so rewarding working with you. Next fall I'll be on a different schedule, though." I say good-bye but later seek her out; frantic, I take both of her hands in mine and say, "You'll still be able to see me, won't you? Three times a week?" "Whatever you want," she says. I nearly faint with relief.*

For the past two years I'd stifled my impulse to greet Dr. Marks on our last session before the summer break with a gift. This year I'd give myself a present: I'd spend July in therapy.

SUMMER

WITH BEN ENROLLED in a nursery school camp for six hours a day, I could devote the month of July to therapy and writing — the book about Ben in the morning, a collection of stories in the afternoon.

This airtight plan suffered from one fatal flaw: I didn't feel like writing. After depositing Ben at camp I found myself dawdling on Broadway, stopping for a bagel, browsing at the stationery store and at Woolworth's, where I invariably came across something I didn't know I needed until I saw it. Home was no haven: a small army of dusty construction workers had recently invaded our building, encasing the exterior walls in flimsy scaffolding, commandeering the elevator to transport hundreds of bricks from roof to basement, and rocking the air shaft with monstrous, breathtaking, heart-stopping clangs and thuds. "Your building is being renovated," read the handwritten signs hung near the mailboxes and washing machines, "Please bear with us." But to those of us home working during the day it seemed as if the building were in fact being demolished.

Ensconced in my study, which also tripled as our bedroom and library, I sat in my chair feeling perfectly blank. My job, especially in comparison to the full-bodied tumult taking place around me, seemed pathetically anemic: while others swung shovels and pickaxes and loaded bricks and swigged beers, I feebly pecked away at a keyboard using only the tips of my fingers and a fraction of my mind. I should have just picked myself up and walked out, gotten away from the lethal, blanketing dust, from the stifling heat of the bedroom. I should have gone shopping, to the beach, to the air-conditioned library, to a ball game, to a hill in Riverside Park where I could eke out an urban suntan. But captive to my own good intentions, I sat at my desk until it was time to fetch Ben or meet with Dr. Marks.

Yet my lethargy contaminated therapy, too; Dr. Marks's air conditioner whirred with the same mind-suctioning frequency as my word processor. Dead-of-summer therapy seemed only marginally familiar, a friend who'd had extensive cosmetic surgery — the same face but with distracting alterations. As at home, I couldn't settle on anything meaty. My manic energy of the spring had deserted me, as it always did after running its course, and I felt only a desultory interest in even the two subjects that last month had begun to obsess me: getting pregnant and moving.

I told Dr. Marks that we'd hired an architect, the same one who had designed Denise's apartment, to see how we could achieve at least the illusion of space, if not more actual room. He'd looked around for about three minutes and told us that short of relocating the front door so that it opened into the living room, turning the entrance alcove into a music room, creating a dining room by partitioning Ben's bedroom, and minimally renovating the kitchen to the tune of ten thousand dollars ("Just the basics," he assured us, new cabinetry and a new floor and new plumbing), he could only advise us to move.

"And for this expertise he charged one hundred and fifty dollars!" I said indignantly, only to find I had nothing else to say. Like Ben, who occasionally emptied all his toys from their respective compartments for no particular reason, I too went on a binge of mental dumping.

But by mid-August I had ground to a complete halt. Never had I felt so isolated; even my closest friendships were suffering. Denise and I had had a senseless fight and had made up only perfunctorily; Monica had scheduled her wedding for a day when I'd still be on vacation and then didn't include Ben in the invitation. I felt as if I lived on the fringe of human fellowship, more out of step and out of synch than I'd felt since childhood. I'd stopped dreaming, stopped writing, phoned almost no one to say good-bye, and felt awkward with Dr. Marks at our last session. I'd be back in three weeks: did my absence constitute a hiatus or just a slightly extended pause?

During the drive north I slept most of the way, confirming my suspicion that I was undergoing a rare, out-of-season hibernation. The Berkshires smacked more of fall than summer. Some of the trees had begun turning, the apple crop was in early, the air had a persistent chill. Ben and I went swimming only twice. I hadn't packed enough sweaters or sweat pants. The restaurants and the music and theater festivals David and I usually enjoyed were all winding down or closing, and tickets and reservations were impossible to secure.

In a way it hardly mattered, for no sooner did we arrive than I was inundated with work. Three editors wanted revisions of articles; two new ideas had occurred to me; and I figured out, during an early morning run, how to write the second chapter of the pregnancy book. In the corner of our downstairs room I set up my antiquated portable typewriter and squirreled myself away, never wanting to leave.

This was supposed to be my vacation. This onslaught of work should have come in July, not now. Should. Never had the word seemed so ridiculous. "I should have followed my instincts; I should have trusted myself," I told Dr. Marks in one of our silent conversations. Two more "shoulds," but perhaps the only true ones.

Yet I found myself sleeping well during those three weeks,

and working well, and finding at every turn that I could exist amid estrangement from friends, that I could work as David relaxed, that I could meet Ben's demands and still work, that I could exist apart from everyone else. I could countenance disputes and desertions and conflicts because there was something enduring in me, something that wasn't the sum of my roles or accomplishments, something that stayed constant and was who I was. The freedom to simply be wasn't a goal or an end, but a starting point.

This vision was most easily sustained in solitude, or in the near solitude I found with Ben. Unable to swim, he was nevertheless drawn to the water's edge. Engineers repairing the dam at the far end of the lake had been steadily lowering the water level all summer, and now it rested at its most shallow point. That part of the shore previously submerged grabbed Ben's attention; delighted, he'd toss rocks, watch other boys fish, study dragonflies for hours. I'd roll up my jeans and join him.

What if the drainage becomes irreversible and the lake unaccountably dries up? I'd ask myself, the very question striking terror in my heart. What if we lose the house? Even in this verdant fold of earth we were not beyond the reach of calamity's thin, icy finger.

"Be careful," I called to Ben, who was intently picking his way along a cluster of boulders dotting the lake bed. That he might lose his balance and fall in didn't seem to occur to him. Likewise, he didn't waste time worrying that financial reverses or new jobs or any amalgam of circumstances could separate him from the house or the lake. He had taken possession of this place, had claimed it, admitted it to his internal landscape. And I had, too. The calm I felt here, the equilibrium, the certainty, didn't inhere in the house or the woods or the lake or the vista; my vision was entirely portable.

"Don't worry, Mom," Ben assured me, "I *am* careful." And he was. Somehow, certainly not by studying me, my son had achieved a perfect balance of caution and adventure. "Anyway," he reminded me with a smile, pausing on a long, flat rock to catch his breath and rest his arms, "the water is so shallow here that even if I fall in I won't get that wet. Come see."

And I did.

THE FOURTH YEAR

I

My father and I are arguing over a key ring with a pre-Revolutionary charm on it; though encrusted with lead, there is an uncut diamond underneath. We both want it; he asks for it but I simply keep my hand extended and say nothing: we both know I'll get it in the end.

"The pre-Revolutionary part is interesting," Dr. Marks said. "What do you make of it?"

"Before my summer revolution," I began, though what had happened over the summer seemed less violent than revelatory — a kind of conversion, a switch of faith or of attention from out there to inside. And inside is a diamond, however disguised. "I suppose I was thinking of the value of a diamond."

"And its toughness," Dr. Marks added.

I smiled. I'd recently learned that a magazine article that I'd had to revise six times had finally been accepted for publication. "For a gentle person, you are very tenacious," said the editor when she phoned with the happy news.

"I can't figure out, though, which one's real; whether I'm really tenacious wrapped in gentleness or the other way 'round."

"Maybe both," Dr. Marks said.

"Maybe," I mused, hearing in my own tone that I wasn't quite as self-disparaging as I'd been, that some of the venom when I talked about my foibles was gone, removed, burned off.

Triumphant news arrived that fall: my pregnancy and motherhood book was sold to a prestigious publishing house. My first book! "But it's not a novel," I hastened to inform Dr. Marks, who had greeted my announcement with just the right amount of happiness.

"Meaning what?" she asked.

"Meaning that I always assumed I'd write a novel, and even though I'm getting published this isn't a novel."

"Is it worse?" she asked.

"Not exactly worse," I said. It was simply less exclusive, less spectacular. Anyone could write a nonfiction book.

"Anyone?"

What did I mean? Was I simply back to my old habit of dismissing whatever I could do well, valuing only that which eluded me?

"I used to write fiction," I said wistfully. "But I haven't in years." That I had this block was one of the reasons I first wanted to come to therapy; I'd written about my frustration in the application essay I'd submitted to the Institute, but somehow the subject hadn't come up, until now. "Actually, my first story was about a daughter who changes her mother. I was worried that my mother would feel threatened. But after she read it, she said, 'That woman and I are nothing alike,' as if she felt shortchanged that I hadn't done a truer portrait."

"It must be hard to write and at the same moment worry about how it's going to be received."

Taped to the light on my desk was an admonition from a former English teacher: "Keep your ass in your chair and your mind on your story." When I told her, Dr. Marks chuckled. "It's hard for me to keep my mind on my story, my eyes on my own paper," I said. "I don't know if I'm afraid of success or afraid of failure —"

"But you're afraid of something," Dr. Marks interrupted.

Yes. When I sat down at my desk with the germ of a story in mind I felt almost literally petrified. "Everyone is full of advice,"

I told Dr. Marks. "Some friends advise me to write about not being able to write. Some tell me to quit therapy, that therapy is why I can't write. You know, if you figure out all your problems you'll have nothing left to work out on paper."

"And what do you think of that?"

"I think that's ridiculous," I said. For one thing, smoothing out life's wrinkles was not what had happened in this room. Therapy didn't offer a pacifier on which to suck; it didn't answer as much as it asked. It was simply one of many routes you could take toward discovering the metaphors, fantasies, and dreams underlying your existence.

"Maybe you're afraid of your fantasies," Dr. Marks offered. "You want to change your mother, your parents, and you can't."

"You should have heard my parents' reaction to the news about my book. They were happy, at first, but then they got caught up in 'Will you need a lawyer for the contract? When will you sign the contract? How does the advance work?' It's as if they simply can't stomach feeling excited."

"Just as you can't. If you could, you wouldn't have to worry that this book isn't a novel."

I smiled, defeated by her relentless honesty.

"There's a difference between being independent and making your parents acknowledge that you are," Dr. Marks said.

"And the former doesn't depend on the latter," I said, finishing her sentence. It seemed I could meet with my editor and conduct our business with my parents' blessing or without it. I could wish for it, could mourn its absence, but I didn't need it. I couldn't spend my life writing scripts for them. They were who they were. That they couldn't rejoice with me as I wished them to didn't mean they didn't love me — they did, just as I loved them and at the same time often bewildered and wounded them.

"Independence was never very prized in your family," Dr. Marks reminded me.

"We gave it lip service," I continued. "And I made the mistake of thinking they meant what they said."

"Can you blame yourself for that? Is it your fault?"

Blame. There was no one to blame — not me, not them. We were who we were. "Fault" became a word suddenly bereft of its meaning: to be angry for what my parents couldn't bestow upon me was like being angry with them for having brown hair instead of red.

During one of my earliest sessions with Dr. Marks, more than three years before, I'd had a dream about my mother in which her face was averted. *"See me!"* I cried to her. "See me as I am." But she couldn't. The ensuing abandonment cascaded over me with staggering force, occasioning not only the first tears I'd shed in therapy but also my first inkling that the relationship I'd entered into with Dr. Marks was somehow wild, uncontrollable, unpredictable, bone-chilling as a blast of arctic wind snaking its way up the cellar steps through a crack in the insulation. *There are people down there,* I remembered thinking, *they're coming upstairs, they're sitting here in the room with me.*

In nearly four years of therapy I'd been hearing all their voices, their exhortations, their pleas and demands. But in the end we are all separate, Dr. Marks and I, my father and I, my mother and I. We each have to save ourselves — and not just once, but over and over again, many times a day, hundreds of times a year; this is the pain that therapy can't extirpate, the final, unavoidable, anguished cry.

To meet with my editor I had to take the same subway I took each day to work; I wore the same business suit I wore to faculty meetings and carried my well-worn briefcase, yet I felt as if I had borrowed a wardrobe and was traveling in a foreign city. Our meeting went very well, but then I wasn't in the most discriminating mood: the offices of the publishing company and the elegant Indian restaurant my editor had selected for lunch were equally magical, equally memorable. With an hour to spare before having to return home to pick Ben up from day care, I window-shopped on Madison Avenue, stopping in a store that sold expensive lingerie. Suddenly I wanted something silky, something with a touch of lace. To commemorate my meeting, I said to myself, producing my credit card to pay for a ridiculously overpriced, skimpy but luxurious, ecru silk teddy. "I'll wear it home," I told the astonished saleswoman, retreating to the fitting room with a scissors to snip off the plastic tags.

I modeled the teddy for David that evening and he smiled absently — lingerie didn't move him. Undaunted, I began shopping compulsively, obsessively, most often in the break between classes or on my way home from therapy, passing up the earrings, sweaters, and scarves I usually spent money on in favor of items that no one else would notice or care about: fine leather wallets and eyeglass cases and calendar covers; sterling silver keychains; frivolous accessories; satiny undergarments — all private, hidden luxuries for no one's admiration but my own. My generosity cut a deep but narrow swath. Eschewing the toy stores, children's clothing stores, book stores, and music stores, where I usually stocked up on presents for Ben and David and friends, I lavished gifts on no one but myself.

"Soon I'm going to need Shoppers Anonymous," I confessed to Dr. Marks. "I'm spending money like water. It's as if I'm under a spell," I cried. "When will I stop?"

"When you feel like it," Dr. Marks said.

Sure enough, after a four-hour spree in a tasteful midtown beauty salon — I had my fingernails manicured, my toenails pedicured, my legs waxed, my face steamed, massaged, and oiled, and, most unaccountably, my eyelashes dyed ("Better than mascara," the Hungarian woman in white lab coat assured me, though it wasn't) — a small voice inside said, That's enough, not in a reproving or reprimanding way, but quite matter-of-factly. I paid for the services rendered in cash, hung up my pink smock, donned my clothes, and closed the door. Outside, the holiday shopping season was going full tilt but my private binge was very merrily over.

"For once," I explained to Dr. Marks, so flushed with excitement I could hardly speak, "For once I let myself go; I gave myself free rein and found out that I could stop when I'd had enough." It felt as if I'd gone on a mapping expedition into a territory I'd never explored, one lush beyond all imagining, yet I nevertheless found myself eager to return home — not because I was ordered to, but because I wanted to.

"I did spend a small fortune," I added. "Our checking account is in a state of shock."

"Will it recover?" Dr. Marks asked.

I nodded.

"Then it seems a small price to pay, don't you think?"

I am redecorating my house. My mother's beautiful dining room table floats around inside our walls with no place to land. I try to fit it into each room but it doesn't stay put. Suddenly it turns into a small plane. I'm standing on a pier with many other people and the plane approaches; we all fear that it will crash. I am terrified. But at the last moment it becomes a tugboat, enveloped in soft padding, and it lands with no explosion, only a soft thud. We all start to cheer.

"You sound as if you felt very relieved," Dr. Marks said.

"I did. I expected an explosion and none came. It was a wonderful anticlimax."

"You managed to get rid of your mother's table and suffered no reprisals."

"We've been looking at houses," I explained to Dr. Marks after a long pause. I was very uncomfortable talking to her about our earnest house hunting. "David scouts places out after work, and on the weekends Ben and I come with him." I paused. "I want to move; I mean, I know we need the space, especially if we want another child. But the very thought terrifies me. I leave the arrangements to David and then worry that he resents having to do all the legwork himself. I just can't get started."

"But you dream about tables that fly," Dr. Marks said.

In December, to celebrate my parents' nearly back-to-back birthdays and my mother's completion of her chemotherapy regimen, my brother and I decided to throw a party. As we'd anticipated, our parents were not enthusiastic: don't spend money on us, they objected. But my brother and I hung tough — it's too late, we told them, the caterer, cake, and paper goods were already selected. All we needed from them was approval of the guest list, which they gave, reluctantly, on one condition: that we write on the invitations, "Please, no presents."

"Is that possible?" I asked Dr. Marks. "Does anyone really not want presents — I mean really, deep down?" This was a genre of question I asked frequently. Was there anyone who wasn't as jealous as I was, or as envious? Was there anyone who really didn't crave attention, who honestly didn't swoon at the sight of a table piled high with presents?

"Not everyone wants to look deep down," she said.

"Well, I'm not going to listen to them," I said. "I sent out the invitations with no such injunction and they'll just have to open their presents and say 'Thank you' the way everyone else does."

"If they don't want pleasure you're going to ram it down their throats," Dr. Marks said, and we both laughed. "Maybe that's how you have to handle deprivation junkies."

"Yes, that's exactly what they are," I said. "And I'm not. Not anymore."

I am in a shower, the water is coursing down over me, a fountain of life; it is ejaculatory, life-giving, and I am doused with happiness.

"The party went really well," I reported at my first session after a two-week break from therapy. "My parents opened their presents almost as eagerly as Ben does his."

Dr. Marks smiled.

I'd also begun to attend an aerobics class one night a week, which to my amazement I thoroughly enjoyed. "They say that for the workout to be effective you have to go more than once a week," I found myself telling Dr. Marks one night. I was often busy after dinner with meetings at Ben's new school and with a writing group I'd recently joined, and my afternoons were filled with teaching and writing. The only other exercise class I could possibly make met on Friday mornings, right in the middle of my therapy appointment.

"So I was thinking about cutting back on therapy one session a week so I could go to this class," I said, finding my hands suddenly fascinating.

"I think that sounds like a good idea," she said.

"Great," I said, tremendously relieved. And I began explaining to her what about the class was so compelling, how liberating it felt to systematically exercise every major muscle group, to dance to the overly loud, pulsating music. Dr. Marks nodded as if to say she understood, but it wasn't until a few hours later, when I was home slicing vegetables, that I paused and realized the source of the bemusement I'd detected in her smile. She wasn't sure that I knew what I was up to, what in fact I had instigated. Therapy was drawing to a close.

My father helps us move to our new home. As a gift he has made us a clock for our mantel. When he brings it over there is another clock, the grandfather clock from his house, inside the one he made for me. The clocks become separate. I put mine by the window. My mother asks if that is the best place for it, and I say, simply, "Yes."

II

ON SATURDAYS that spring, David, Ben, and I would house-hunt. David was in charge of contacting real estate agents, studying the real estate pages in the newspaper, making appointments, and compiling a notebook of facts and figures. I was about as helpful as Ben. Each house we pulled up in front of looked immediately, terribly wrong. Heavy with dread, I could barely heave myself out of the car. To poke through someone's closets, nose around in their kitchens, peruse the contents of their medicine cabinets, and sniff inside their shower stalls was to enter their lives.

"We love this house, we raised our children here but now we have to sell it because my wife had a stroke, she can't take the stairs." "My daughter — did I tell you she's valedictorian of her high school class? — and when she leaves for college, this place will be just too big for my husband and me." "My husband died, and my mother came to live with me and now she died." "My husband lost his job and we want to relocate in California." Stories rattled around drafty hallways, clung to the carpet like the ineradicable odor of cigarette smoke in the upholstery or milk gone bad in the back of the refrigerator, adhering to the house's inhabitants as they shuffled after us from room to room, and flocking to me as if I were wearing a sign that said, Tell me. Sometimes I cleared my throat to ask about the tax rate or the utility bills, but no one was fooled; my contribution was to stay

mute and immobile in the face of flux, the imperturbable lis-
tener.

"This is our opportunity to make a change," David would ex-
hort me, invigorated by the very crossroads at which we stood
and which so intimidated me. Sometimes he must have thought
me somnambulant, and he spoke as if he wanted to shake me
by the shoulders, slap my cheeks: "You have to get the big picture." But I was hopelessly stuck on the close-ups, for each
house for sale depicted a family in crisis. Even those young
couples for whom moving on meant moving up, whose
halfhearted, slapdash attempts at decorating hadn't concealed
their impatience or their certainty that they could do better than
this, were at a crossroads. I studied the bric-a-brac cluttering a
mantel; the chartreuse rug blanketing an entire house from
basement to attic; the bathroom whose four walls, ceiling, and
floor were mirrored; all the beautiful keepsakes and thousands
of little-awful-uglies, which piqued my covetousness or my disdain, which someone would pack or discard. Gaping at the possessions of strangers, I silently inventoried my own: the ceramic
bowl we hated and never used, the wedding present from the
relatives in Florida, what did it say about us? Would we take it
with us if we moved, or chuck it?

In one house, a pleasant Cape Cod on a corner lot in a good
school district, hung a cuckoo clock, and written upon its face
in black Gothic letters was my mother's maiden name — a co-
incidence in which I delighted. Could I live here?

"This house just went on the market this morning and it
won't last the day," the real estate agent cautioned us, noting,
perhaps, the dreamy look in my eyes. He was enormously fat
and getting in and out of our little car required minutes of grunt-
ing effort. He shepherded us to several other houses, all hope-
less, and two hours later we found ourselves back at the Cape.
"They've had a few offers," he whispered to us on now heavily
trafficked stairs. In a matter of minutes we'd signed a binder and

left a personal check as a deposit. We had forty-eight hours in which to make up our minds.

"That was the breakthrough for me, I think," I told Dr. Marks at our next appointment, two days after we'd let the binder lapse and had our check returned. "I don't know how, but suddenly something shifted into focus. It's not that I suddenly want to move," I elaborated, "but rather I had a vision of what it would be like in five years to be exactly where we are now. I'd feel as if we were stagnating. We'd be doubly cramped and crabby — David already feels completely claustrophobic in our apartment — so I guess this is just the time to do it."

I still couldn't imagine my kitchen table positioned in a breakfast nook or my framed antique quilt squares hanging in a dining room, but maybe I didn't have to, not yet. Ben assumed that whatever he saw in any house — including and especially the toys of the various children — would remain; moving to him signified less a break with the past than a fortuitous inheritance. Perhaps I had to begin by imagining that the house we would buy would come with all its possessions still in place: all I had to do was wake up and begin living there.

I am cleaning a patchwork quilt I made by spraying cleaning fluid on it. As I watch, the colors begrimed by dirt and time come alive, but when I get to the very top layer the colors stay dull and lifeless.

Dr. Marks smiled when I related the dream. "Something still scares you about moving," she said.

"Everything scares me. I don't even think we can afford it. We'll have to borrow money from our parents, for one thing."

"Did they offer to lend it to you?"

"Yes, they want us to move. My father has wanted us to move to a house for years. He can't understand why we've waited so long. But I wish we could manage it ourselves."

"Do you think they would ask for something in return?"

"No, nothing like that. It's just, I've spent all this time trying

to separate from them, to live on my own, and here I am needing them again."

"You can need them for certain things and not everything,"
Dr. Marks reminded me. "If it would make them happy to see
you in a house, and if that's what you want, then it seems as if
accepting the loan wouldn't compromise the independence
you've achieved."

These days Dr. Marks acted more like the older sister I'd always wanted than the therapist I'd grappled with. Much of the
resonance I'd always heard behind her words, my sense that she
was a screen behind which I saw the shadows of many people,
was gone. Now she was someone who knew about all of my
secrets and would never, ever betray me.

"It's not just that," I protested. At the bottom of my broom
closet sat a small metal toolbox, a gift from my father. Within
was one hammer, one screwdriver, one wrench, and a package
of thumbtacks. "Neither David nor I is handy; neither of us is
particularly interested in becoming so. To undertake the commitment of keeping up a house, not to mention the financial
commitment," my voice trailed off as I realized what I was really
saying. Undertaking this commitment — any commitment —
was agonizing. I hung back until the last possible second, afraid
the water was too cold, the distance too far, my foothold too
precarious, even as the beach eroded around me and the sail-
boat just offshore beckoned. But how could I dive in? My
friends were all in the city, as was my job, Ben's school, all my
professional connections. And so was Dr. Marks.

*A flood advances up Broadway. As I head to a subway a fire truck passes
and instructs all pedestrians to move uptown. I start to panic — I don't
know where Ben and David are. Then the panic abates. We live on the
top floor, I remind myself, which means we will be safe.*

"In other words," Dr. Marks suggested, "what may be harm-
ful to others may not necessarily harm you and yours."

"I suppose," I said, noncommittally, unable to shake the sense that by moving out of the city I was perpetrating an act of disloyalty against all my friends.

"I wonder if you also feel that way about therapy too," Dr. Marks asked.

It was true. I hadn't yet brought up the fact that moving would mean the end of therapy as well, for wherever we moved would be far enough away to make regular meetings problematic. "You always said that I was going to be the one to end therapy this time, not you." Dr. Marks nodded. "Now I feel as if I'm letting things end therapy instead of making a decision."

"You decided to take your exercise class. And you're deciding to move for the good of your family and yourself. That certainly sounds like a decision."

I still wasn't convinced. Why, after four years of therapy, wasn't I able to march in and trumpet my resolve? Why did I still feel as if I slithered in and out of situations? Why did I have to embed momentous decisions in prattle about aerobics classes? Wasn't therapy supposed to alter all that?

Or was that asking too much? Was I acting as if my personality were a plain brown skirt I'd brought in for lengthening, only to be disappointed when the expert tailor merely followed my instructions instead of magically transforming it into a glamorous evening gown or an eye-catching cocktail dress?

"I had a dream about sitting in a movie theater with you," I told Dr. Marks. "It was the movie of a woman's life, and when it was over I said to you, 'There's an accomplished, competent, busy, capable woman.' Only the woman was me. I can only appreciate what I do when I think of it in the abstract. Up close, I always feel as if I'm struggling, suffocating; I can only see what I can't do."

"Then you have to go to the movies more often," Dr. Marks said.

I had learned to take her glib-sounding comments seriously.

For she was right: Therapy hadn't cured the sickening dread with which I greeted any hint of change. But thanks to therapy this initial reaction didn't prevail. Now I could go to the movies, put on a new pair of glasses, and see my situation from a wholly different perspective; in fact, very often, the same constellation of factors which threatened to overwhelm could, in a different light, make me feel exceptionally competent and challenged. Yes, moving would open a new chapter of our lives. So would ending therapy. I had to trust that Dr. Marks wouldn't send me off unless she felt that I was ready.

"The woman in the movie is shocked that she doesn't miss coming to therapy three times a week," I said tentatively.

"I don't see how she'd have a second to miss anything," Dr. Marks replied.

David's parents offered to take Ben for the weekend so David and I could get away. I wrote to hotels and inns, sketched out routes and itineraries, but our plans never solidified and in the end David and I stayed in the city, spending the weekend the way we used to before Ben was born. Relieved of our responsibilities, stripped of obligations, we quite naturally fell into our old rhythms, eating in a funky Cuban-Chinese restaurant, walking down Broadway to catch a movie, stopping for ice cream, dropping in on friends. But the ease with which we slid back into our routines didn't counteract our unspoken yet shared feeling that lifetimes had passed since we last felt this free.

Trying to decide which dress to wear for the highlight of our weekend — Saturday night dinner at an Indian restaurant and a chamber music concert at Carnegie Hall — I sat down on the edge of Ben's neatly made bed as if he were tucked into it, awaiting his good-night kiss. David was dressing in our bedroom; Miles Davis's version of "Bye Bye Blackbird" played on the stereo in the light of late afternoon. Suddenly, almost acrobatically, I swung up my legs and slipped under the covers.

Ben will sleep in this bed until he leaves for college, I thought; Ben, my son, the reason I went into therapy, or so I once thought; Ben, who was right now most present in his absence, whose toys we didn't have to pick out of the couch or tub, with whom we didn't have to negotiate for rights to the television; Ben, whom I never had the luxury of missing, for I'd never been away from him long enough; Ben, without whom life seemed unimaginable no matter how much I was savoring every sweet solitary moment of this honeymoon weekend.

I closed my eyes. In our bedroom David began loading his pockets with change, credit cards, keys, guitar picks. I remembered the sounds emanating from my parents' bedroom before one of their evenings out, my father's crisp scratchings and janglings, my mother's rustlings and smoothings, inexplicable sounds, which took place out of sight, almost out of earshot. Tantalizing grown-up sounds. From this slit between door and jamb Ben glimpsed the after-dark and early-morning goings-on of his parents. Here he lay, night after night and morning after morning, wondering what it felt like to be an adult, not knowing — how could he? — that in the next room his mother was asking herself the very same question.

I am watching the last episode of a television program I love, a program about police in the inner city. The camera pans through the precinct and I see all the familiar faces except one, the captain, my favorite character. He is not there.

"The key person missing may be you," Dr. Marks said. "You think your role is to protect others, as the police do by their presence, only the way you protect others is by not being there."

"By not bringing my demands into the picture."

She nodded.

"Sometimes I think I just experience myself as a bag of demands, or as someone who is either praised or criticized, but not someone who exists in an abiding way."

"You protect yourself that way," Dr. Marks said.

"What do you mean?"

"That's how you keep yourself from wanting, from being disappointed, from moving on."

"Or moving away." I paused. "You know, I never knew how bad I was at saying hello until you showed me," I said. "But I always knew I was terrible at good-bye. My version of saying good-bye is to promise to write. And I do. To everyone. Old boyfriends, old colleagues, people I never even cared about that much. Saying good-bye sounds unbearably final. And I'm wondering how in the world I'm going to say good-bye to you."

"Maybe you don't have to. I'd like us to stay in touch."

"You *would*?"

"I'm very interested in what happens to you." She studied me. "You seem surprised."

"I'm just remembering when I used to dream about meeting in a restaurant for coffee, coming over, seeing what your apartment looks like."

She laughed. "Your old fantasy."

"Only now I don't care what your living room looks like, or how you drink your coffee. Back then these details seemed so crucial. And now I can't even remember why."

But on the way home I figured it out. I knew Dr. Marks in the only way I needed to know her, and trusted that she knew me; our sense of each other would not yellow, or fray, or need revision or updating in the light of new information. Even after I stopped seeing her she would know me. Our relationship existed in an enduring way, tucked into a fold of the present moment in whose existence I had never before — not for one second — believed.

III

"My life is taking over," I cried in mock seriousness. Events were happening at breakneck speed. Over the weekend we'd seen an affordable house we liked in a promising neighborhood, the first house I had felt any urgency about owning. With our parents we engaged in long, forthright financial discussions during which David consulted his notebook, made quick computations involving ridiculously huge sums of money, and concluded that with their help the house was within our grasp. In a matter of days we had gone to contract and had a troop of lawyers, agents, and bankers working for us.

"And right in the middle of all these negotiations I'm hip-deep in infertility procedures, taking my temperature, filling out charts, testing my urine to determine the optimal thirty-six-hour period for conception. Very romantic." Dr. Marks smiled sympathetically.

"Wait, I'm not finished. Just last night we found out, my mother has to go back into the hospital again. And in the middle of all this I'm trying to end therapy."

Only a year ago the surface of my life had seemed so calm — my flirtations causing the barest ripple on the otherwise still waters of work and family — while therapy ran deep and wild. Yet now the currents had reversed, and Dr. Marks's office was an ocean of serenity in the midst of an eddying reality. "Real life," I kept remarking to Dr. Marks, "real life is attacking me."

"It tends to do that," she said. "You can call me if you need to, any time" — an offer she'd never before tendered. I was so grateful I couldn't respond beyond nodding; I even had to avert my eyes.

I am in the midst of a dinner party. I have served everyone and have put a portion at my place, but I must leave the dining room for a moment to tend to something in the kitchen. When I return I find that one of my friend's sons has climbed into my seat and is eating my food. I look at the serving dish, but it is empty. "He took what belonged to me." I cry bitterly, inconsolably.

Immediately upon jolting awake, I began rehearsing, memorizing the dream even as consciousness fragmented it, desperately trying to fix it on a mental slide to examine under the microscope of therapy. It was like discovering a stratum of rock beneath what I had assumed was bedrock, or finding a fossil whose very antiquity necessitated the formulation of a more distant past: everything inside me, this dream told me, was immeasurably older and unspeakably deeper than I knew.

"On one level, I suppose the dream is about the birth of my brother," I told Dr. Marks. "But it also seems as if the feeling in the dream predates my brother's birth, that it exists somewhere in my very bones. But we talked about all my feelings of deprivation ages ago. Why is it coming back now?"

"Maybe because the dinner party is almost over."

"You mean therapy." I chewed that over, thinking that at this moment therapy resembled nothing so much as a controlled free-fall that allowed me to follow the images of my dreams down their twisty chutes and land in a subterranean world as drafty, leaky, and dangerous as an abandoned mine that should have caved in years ago but hadn't. Before Dr. Marks lent me a lamp and her hand, I'd never known that this place existed within me, denying the tremors it set loose in much the same way as people living within earthquake zones do.

Yet knowing of this chamber's existence and location didn't irrevocably brighten its gloom, cure its dampness, or neuter its dangers. It would always be there, and occasionally I would tumble in, claw my way out, and fall back in. At least I had a lamp now, the kind excavators use, a hand-held torch with a bulb, encased by wire mesh, whose beam illuminated a modest circular skirt of ground: I could see only a few steps behind me and a few in front, but somehow that seemed a lifesaving advantage.

"I'm going away for two weeks after the Fourth of July," Dr. Marks said. We were both hunched over our date books.

"And we're leaving for the Berkshires in early August," I said, our valiant effort to squeeze in a two-week vacation before moving later that month.

"So I guess that means that our last appointment will have to be —"

"July 30," I said. "The end," I wrote in my calendar.

A lovely man wearing a tweed jacket wants me to take a walk with him. No, I tell myself, I won't do it; I don't want to shoulder his enormous need. He may be disappointed in me, may leave me, but I know I won't be alone.

On my way to therapy on July 30 I stopped at the florist and purchased ten long-stemmed red roses, which I presented to Dr. Marks the moment I stepped into her office.

They were astonishingly perfect flowers in full bloom. "You can't possibly be surprised," I said. This was exactly the gift I'd told her I'd stopped short of bringing her every summer since I'd first begun seeing her. Yet she seemed genuinely moved, and scurried about her office filling a vase, arranging the flowers and ferns, and selecting a perfect spot to place them.

I settled myself on the couch. The point of the session had

already been accomplished, it seemed. Still, the air was scented with unreality. This was the last time I'd sit on this couch in this position facing this woman. She'd be here, but I wouldn't. My eyes misted, and then I was crying. It wasn't that we didn't have much to say, but I had the sense that our conversation would never be over.

"Moving is a strange experience," I said, just to start talking, for nothing could happen, I knew, until I said the first word. I'd lived for ten years in the apartment I was now vacating, longer than I'd lived in any single residence, even during childhood. During the seven years between leaving for college and moving in with David, I'd moved often, sometimes yearly. To combat the rootlessness I'd assembled a cache of keepsakes — letters, photos, diaries — a kind of personal, portable shrine I could easily pack, tote, and stash in the night table of whatever bedroom I happened to be occupying. But when I'd come across the familiar box just last night, I'd been overcome with sadness: the box hadn't been touched in ten years. Many of the people whose letters had comforted me, whose words had granted continuity in the face of change, had become shadows in my life. I didn't even know where some of them were living.

"I still wish I were the kind of person who could just walk out, take nothing but essentials, and begin again." Out of the corner of my eye appeared the image of the woman I always wanted to be, the one who walked breezily through life, who exuded a confidence I always lacked, a sureness that always put others at ease. She carried everything she needed in her purse. I hadn't become her, as I had once hoped I would, but she seemed on the verge of stopping to talk. Maybe all I had to do was call out to her. In her arms she held a bouquet of roses.

Dr. Marks and I watched the time wind down, much as we had during our first session. I fumbled around for my pocketbook; when I looked up she was already standing, and we embraced. "Keep in touch," she said.

"I'll send you a card with my new address and phone."

"You know where to find me. And thank you again for the flowers."

"Thank you," I said, meaning for everything, and with that I let go of her hands and turned away, walking through the empty suite and out into the brilliant, steamy sunshine. I headed toward Broadway to catch the bus but when I finally looked up I found that I had in fact walked all the way home.

AFTERWORD

"Dr. Marks called you," David said casually when I returned home from work one afternoon. As if he had relayed a message from my lover, my heart quickened and my face flushed. Since we'd moved I'd sent Dr. Marks a change of address card and had heard nothing in return. "She said you could call her back tonight or tomorrow night after nine." I remembered the fall evening four years ago when mine was her last appointment and we'd met outside the Institute across from Central Park, each hoping to hail a cab home in the early darkness.

On the phone, as soon as she said "Hello," her voice conjured up every room we'd ever sat in, every conversation we'd ever had: I knew its inflections and tone as intimately as I did David's. We chatted at first — she asked after my mother, who was in good health, about the house, my new job — as if we were friends getting back in touch after a few weeks of silence.

What she had called about was an insurance matter. We cleared that up easily.

"How are you doing?" she asked. I told her that adjusting to the new house was easier than I had thought; all the trauma seemed to have preceded our move and everything since had been surprisingly, blessedly easy. I told her I'd begun writing, tentatively, about my experiences in therapy.

"I'd be very interested to see what comes of that project," she said. "I was an English major too, you know." I didn't. She also told me that she'd begun doing some writing herself, mainly book reviews.

"Send me some," I suggested.

"Oh, they're nothing, really," she protested, but agreed, finally, to put one or two in the mail.

"It's funny," I said, "because sometimes I think about going back to school to become a therapist. Maybe we should just trade credentials for a while."

"Good idea," she said, laughing. "But in the meantime, drop me a note now and then. Let me know how you're doing."

"I will," I said, though I felt as if we were constantly in touch, as if she were inside me, just as my writing students learned to internalize an editor, as Ben was learning to internalize me. Her voice piped up whenever I needed help making a decision or allowing myself a moment's pleasure, or simply to remind me that there were other, less paralyzing or hurtful ways to view a situation that left me stymied. Almost as if I'd swallowed her, she informed my dialogue with myself. That she still sat in her office and helped other clients and became involved in their lives as she had in mine — helped them out of crises and into understanding — didn't wound but rather soothed me. She had taught me to live with paradox and contradiction and uncertainty. From her I had learned that there is no truth, no self, only truths and selves; with her companionship I could venture to traverse the mystifying distances from one to the other.

Therapy seemed both a journey and a cycle through which I gained an understanding of myself, enabling me — for now — to get on with my life. That this understanding might be supplanted or change or prove incomplete didn't matter: I couldn't have gotten here — to this actual or internal address — without her.

What could I tell her? My feelings about her were deeper than affection, than awe, than gratitude. I'd been seduced, loved, transfigured, and now released. Therapy, I realized, was the story of a love affair.

"I'll try to write too," Dr. Marks said. "It's hard for me to find time, but know that I think of you."

I closed my eyes. "I think of you too," I said. "I think of you every day."